Data Monetization

Driving Quantifiable Financial Benefits from Enterprise Data Management

Sunil Soares
Mark Gallman
Alex Scroggins
Pamela Taylor

Information Asset LLC
Harrington Park, NJ
www.information-asset.com

Data Monetization: Driving Quantifiable Financial Benefits from Enterprise Data Management
by Sunil Soares, Mark Gallman, Alex Scroggins, and Pamela Taylor

First Edition

Information Asset, LLC
Harrington Park, NJ
USA
www.information-asset.com

YourDataConnect, LLC
Harrington Park, NJ
USA
yourdataconnect.com

ISBN: 978-0-578-76153-4

About the Authors

Sunil Soares is the chief executive officer of Information Asset, a consulting firm that specializes in helping organizations build out their data monetization programs. He is also chief executive officer of YourDataConnect, a software solutions firm focused on data monetization. Prior to this role, Sunil was director of information governance at IBM, where he worked with clients across six continents and multiple industries. Before joining IBM, Sunil consulted with major financial institutions at the Financial Services Strategy Consulting Practice of Booz Allen & Hamilton in New York. Sunil lives in New Jersey and holds an MBA in Finance and Marketing from the University of Chicago Booth School of Business.

Sunil is the author of several books, including *The IBM Data Governance Unified Process*, *Selling Information Governance to the Business: Best Practices by Industry and Job Function*, *Big Data Governance*, *IBM InfoSphere: A Platform for Big Data Governance and Process Data Governance*, *Data Governance Tools*, *The Chief Data Officer Handbook for Data Governance*, *Data Governance Guide for BCBS 239 and DFAST Compliance*, and *Data Sovereignty and Enterprise Data Management: Extending Beyond the European Union General Data Protection Regulation.*

Mark Gallman is a principal consultant at Information Asset. Mark helps clients build, implement, and operationalize enterprise data governance and data management programs, working with cross-functional stakeholders in developing policies and standards to meet business, legal, and regulatory requirements and creating processes and procedures to drive adherence. Prior to this role, Mark was director of financial systems and data governance at CDK Global (formerly ADP Dealer Services), a division of a Fortune® 500® company, specializing in integrated technology and digital marketing. Mark has more than 25 years of global financial and data management experience with large multinational software, manufacturing, and services companies.

Pamela Taylor, CDMP, is a managing director with Information Asset. In this role, she focuses on providing support and guidance to leaders of organizations in the operationalization of data capabilities. Pam excels in developing and defining necessary standards and policies aligned to a data strategy. Pam is a strong advocate for data and information stewardship; she believes that this foundational concept reinforces enterprise data and information governance.

Prior to her role at Information Asset, Pam was vice president of data governance and quality at TD Bank, where she was an integral part of the office of the chief data officer and aided in successful OCC and FRB examinations. Before joining the bank, Pam was the chief data steward at Independence Blue Cross, a health insurance payer. In this role, Pam drove enterprise data governance and the maturity of corporate reference data.

Pam has over 12 years of experience in data governance, with increasingly senior roles. This experience ranges from evaluating solutions at program levels as well as on an enterprise scope with a focus on long-term return on investment. Pam has served on expert panels and has presented at DAMA chapter events and Master Data Management & Governance Summits. She is an active member of DAMA International and president of the board of directors for DAMA Philadelphia/Delaware Valley Chapter.

Alex Scroggins is chief technology officer with YourDataConnect™, a software-as-a-service (SaaS) data monetization platform. In this role, he focuses on overseeing the product management and development of the YourDataConnect™ platform. Alex is a six-time certified Salesforce® architect and has 15 years of experience in software architecture and development, systems integration, data warehousing, business intelligence, data governance, and data management.

Contents

About the Authors iii

Preface ix

Chapter 1: Introduction to Data Monetization 1

Business Outcomes of Data Monetization 1

Data Monetization Is a Cross-Functional Discipline 2

Enterprise Data Management 2

Technology 5

Legal Engineering 6

Finance 6

Operationalizing Data Monetization 7

1. Identify Stakeholders 7
2. Build an Inventory of Use Cases 8
3. Develop Business Cases 8

4. Execute Initiatives 9

5. Realize Business Benefits 9

Summary 10

Chapter 2: Identify Stakeholders 11

Identify Lines of Business 11

Identify Divisions or Departments 11

Summary 12

Chapter 3: Build Inventory of Use Cases 13

Identify Use Cases 13

Sample Use Case to Increase Revenues 15

Sample Use Case to Reduce Costs 15

Sample Use Case to Manage Risk 16

Use Case Inventory Template 16
Linking and Prioritizing Use Cases to Strategic Objectives 16
Summary 17

Chapter 4: Develop Business Cases 19
Start with Use Case 19
Identify Business Case Drivers 19
Compute Estimated Financial Benefits 20
Data Monetization Dashboard 21
Summary 24

Chapter 5: Execute Initiatives 25
Define Business Rules 25
Implement Business Rules in Data Quality Tool 26
Assess and Remediate Data 26
Summary 29

Chapter 6: Realize Business Benefits 31
Data Monetization Dashboard 31
Data Monetization Traceability 32
Summary 33

Chapter 7: Legal Engineering 35
Summary 36

Chapter 8: Sensitive Data Management 37
Heightened Focus on Security and Privacy 37
Sensitive Data 37
European Union General Data Protection Regulation 38
California Consumer Privacy Act 39
Children's Online Privacy Protection Act 42
Video Privacy Protection Act 42
Video Privacy Protection Act 43
Summary 43

Chapter 9: Consumer Protection Law 45
Consumer Financial Protection Bureau 45
Community Reinvestment Act 46
Consumer Leasing Act 50
Electronic Fund Transfer Act 52
Equal Credit Opportunity Act 52
Fair Credit Reporting Act 55
Fair Debt Collection Practices Act 57
Gramm-Leach-Bliley Act 57
Home Mortgage Disclosure Act 60
Homeowners Protection Act 63
Real Estate Settlement Procedures Act 64
Secure and Fair Enforcement for Mortgage Licensing Act 65
Truth in Lending Act 66
Truth in Savings Act 68
Unfair, Deceptive, or Abusive Acts or Practices 69
Summary 70

Chapter 10: Financial Services Regulations 71
Bank Secrecy Act/Anti-Money Laundering 71
Comprehensive Capital Analysis and Review 74
Current Expected Credit Loss 76
Office of Foreign Assets Control 80
Financial Crimes Enforcement Network 82
Summary 83

Chapter 11: Life Sciences Regulations 85
Identification of Medicinal Products 85
European Union Medical Device Regulation 89
United States Food and Drug Administration UDI Final Rule 90
Summary 90

Chapter 12: Data Marketplace 91
Data Marketplace Personas 91
Publisher Persona 92
Administrator Persona 93
Subscriber Persona 93
Regulatory Compliance 94
Internal Data Sharing 95
External Data Sharing 97
Data Valuation 97
Differential Rules of Visibility 98
Summary 99

Chapter 13: YourDataConnect Overview 101
Data Monetization Dashboard 102
Dashboard 102
Business Glossary 103
Data Catalog 105
Data Privacy 106
Workflows 107
Reference Data Management 110
Regulatory Compliance 110
Summary 112

Appendix A: Glossary 113
Appendix B: Acronyms 117

Preface

Data monetization is a cross-functional discipline that leverages data and information to expose opportunities to generate revenue, reduce cost, and manage risks. Data literacy underpins the ability to identify the use cases to support a successful data monetization initiative. We define data literacy as the maturation an individual acquires as a result of extensive study and understanding of what data means by reading, understanding, and communicating data as information.

Data monetization is often related to direct selling or data insights. Throughout this book, the focus will shift to indirect data monetization. Revenue generation can be linked to revenue insights that determine where an organization may uncover opportunities for internal, partner, and customer revenue growth. By improving the understanding of customer trends, organizations can enhance the customer experience and strengthen loyalty.

Cost reduction is also an important aspect of data monetization in terms of retiring applications and removing redundant expenses.

Tapping into foundational disciplines of enterprise data management, data quality, architecture, and data quality management effectively is a proven technique that not only optimizes data use and improves data sharing and reuse but also reduces costs, thereby monetizing data for the organization.

In today's ever-changing regulatory environment, risk reduction and management is paramount for most organizations. Data monetization strategies to improve compliance within regulatory landscapes that focus on the enforcement of access controls or provide control over the approved use of data are a part of what we describe in the legal engineering discipline that makes up data monetization.

This book is geared toward business users and provides a framework for data monetization. The book includes references to software tools, wherever applicable, and provides insight for the following roles:

- Chief Data Officer
- Chief Financial Officer
- Compliance
- Enterprise Data Management Lead
- Enterprise Information Management Lead
- Data Governance Lead
- Data Steward

1

Introduction to Data Monetization

Enterprise data management (EDM) programs have lacked business adoption due to a limited tie-in with financial benefits. Organizations have generally found it extremely difficult to get senior management buy-in in the absence of regulatory pressures or the fear of a data breach. Data monetization is an approach to drive quantifiable business benefits from data and information. This bottom-line–driven approach is key to generating business adoption with stakeholders.

> ***Data monetization*** is a cross-functional discipline that draws from best practices in enterprise data management, technology, legal engineering, and finance to leverage data to increase revenues, reduce costs, and manage risk.

Business Outcomes of Data Monetization

Data monetization has three broad outcomes:

- *Grow revenues*—Data monetization drives an increase in the organization's revenues. For example, a retailer improves cross-sell and up-sell opportunities based on a single view of the household.
- *Reduce costs*—Data monetization facilitates overall cost reduction efforts. For example, a manufacturer improves the quality of billing addresses to reduce accounts receivable balances and net working capital.
- *Manage risk*—Data monetization supports risk mitigation efforts. For example, a bank reduces credit risk by establishing a unified view of counterparty risk across affiliates and subsidiaries.

Data Monetization Is a Cross-Functional Discipline

Data monetization is a cross-functional discipline that draws from best practices in enterprise data management, technology, legal engineering, and finance (Figure 1.1).

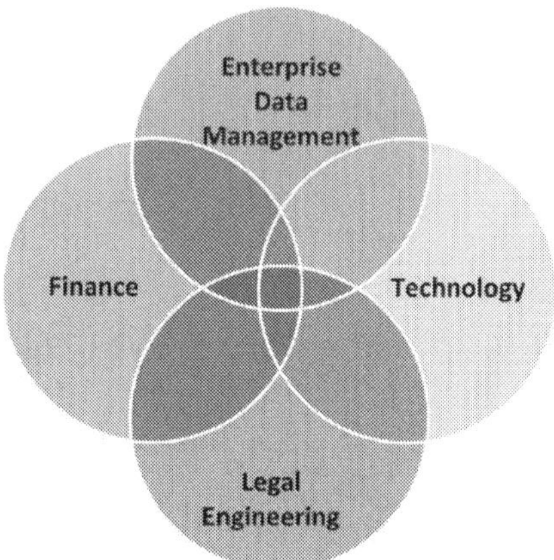

Figure 1.1: Data monetization is a cross-functional discipline

Enterprise Data Management

EDM refers to the ability of an organization to precisely define, easily integrate, and effectively retrieve data for both internal applications and external communication.[1] It includes a number of disciplines, such as data governance, data architecture, data modeling, data integration (extract, transform, load, or ETL), data security, data privacy, master data management, reference data management, data warehousing and business intelligence, information lifecycle management, content management, metadata management, data quality management, data ownership and stewardship, and critical data elements (CDEs) and critical data sets. Strictly speaking, data security and privacy are broader disciplines but have significant interdependencies with enterprise data management and data governance.

---

[1] Wikipedia, "Enterprise data management," http://en.wikipedia.org/wiki/Enterprise_data_management

As shown in Figure 1.2, data governance is a foundational program that ties together the other EDM disciplines.

Figure 1.2: The EDM disciplines that contribute to comprehensive data governance

We discuss each EDM discipline below:

- *Data governance*—The formulation of policy to optimize, secure, and leverage information as an enterprise asset by aligning the objectives of multiple functions.
- *Data architecture*—A discipline that sets data standards for data systems as a vision or a model of the eventual interactions between those data systems.[2]
- *Data modeling*—The process of establishing data models, which use a set of symbols and text to precisely explain a subset of real

---

[2] Wikipedia, "Data architecture," http://en.wikipedia.org/wiki/Data_architecture

information to improve communication within the organization and thereby lead to a more flexible and stable application environment.[3]

- *Data integration*—A process that involves combining data from multiple sources to provide new insights to business users.
- *Data security*—The process of avoiding unauthorized access to data.
- *Data privacy*—The process that involves protecting data belonging to an individual or organization. Privacy is the "right to be left alone," as defined in a *Harvard Law Review* article called "The Right to Privacy" written in 1890 by Justice Louis Brandeis and Samuel Warren.[4] Subsequent regulations and legislation around the world have built on this definition.
- *Master data management*—The process of establishing a single version of the truth for an organization's critical data entities, such as customers, products, materials, vendors, and chart of accounts.
- *Reference data management*—The process of managing static data such as country codes, state or province codes, and industry classification codes, which may be placed in lookup tables for reference by other applications across the enterprise.
- *Data warehousing and business intelligence*—The process of creating a centralized repository of data for reporting and analysis.
- *Information lifecycle management*—The process and methodology of managing information through its lifecycle, from creation through disposal, including compliance with legal, regulatory, and privacy requirements.
- *Content management*—The process of digitizing, collecting, and classifying paper and electronic documents.
- *Metadata management*—The management of information that describes the characteristics of any data artifact, such as its name, location, criticality, quality, business rules, and relationships to other data artifacts.
- *Data quality management*—A discipline that includes methods to measure and improve the quality and integrity of an organization's data.

---

[3] Steve Hoberman, *Data Modeling Made Simple*, 2nd ed., Technics Publications, LLC, 2009
[4] Susan E. Gallagher, "Context," http://faculty.uml.edu/sgallagher/harvard__law_review.htm

- *Data ownership and stewardship*—The process of identifying individuals who will be accountable for the trustworthiness, as well as supporting the security and privacy, of data within their purview.
- *Critical data elements and critical data sets*—In the context of data sovereignty, critical data elements and critical data sets (groupings or collections of data) are data that may cause operational, regulatory, or financial risk if they are not collected or are incorrect, compromised, or used inappropriately.

Technology

Technology is critical to the successful implementation of a data monetization program. YourDataConnect™ supports a data monetization dashboard to provide a high-level summary of opportunities to use data in order to grow revenues, reduce costs, and mitigate risks; each one of these opportunities has a potential value that is calculated by YourDataConnect, as well as workflows to actualize the potential value (Figure 1.3).

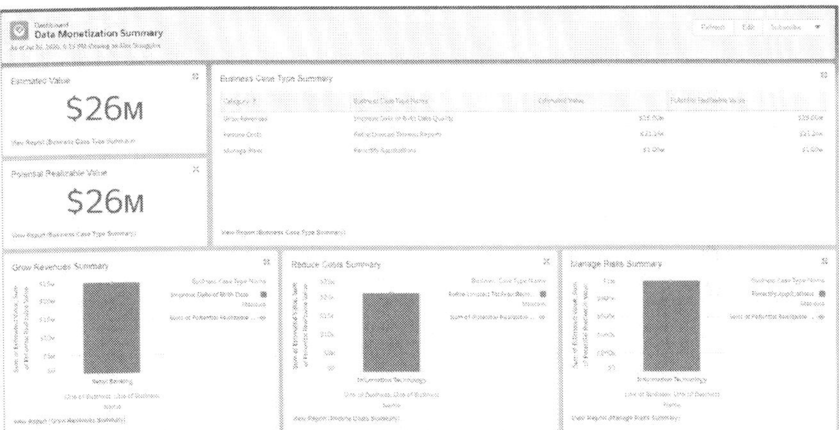

Figure 1.3: YourDataConnect™ data monetization summary dashboard

Legal Engineering

Legal engineers use their legal knowledge combined with technological know-how and project management experience to optimize existing products, services, and processes but also to create new solutions to specific problems faced by clients, using a combination of technology and tools.[5]

The European Union's (EU's) General Data Protection Regulation (GDPR) is a recent example of a regulation that requires legal engineering. The GDPR applies to the processing of personal data of all data subjects, including customers, employees, and prospects. Non-compliance with the GDPR may result in huge fines, which can be the higher of €20M or 4 percent of the organization's worldwide revenues. GDPR legal engineers need to consider strategies to anonymize personal data to be compliant with the regulation. Other examples of regulations that require legal engineering include Australia's Privacy Act, the Russian Personal Data Localization law, the People's Republic of China's (PRC's) Cybersecurity Law, and Canada's Anti-Spam Legislation (CASL).

Finance

Successful data monetization requires quantification of the financial benefits of enterprise data management initiatives in terms of reducing costs, growing revenues, and managing risk. For example, a data monetization project may improve the data quality for customer bill-to addresses at a manufacturing company. Finance needs to sign off on the financial benefits derived from reducing accounts receivable float and net working capital.

---

[5] HighQ, part of Thomson Reuters, "The rise of the legal engineer," July 27, 2016, https://www.lexology.com/library/detail.aspx?g=f8d9bb92-3779-4bc2-9f1b-7354d416acb1#:~:text=Legal%20engineers%20use%20their%20legal,combination%20of%20technology%20and%20tools

Operationalizing Data Monetization

Successful data monetization involves five steps (Figure 1.4).

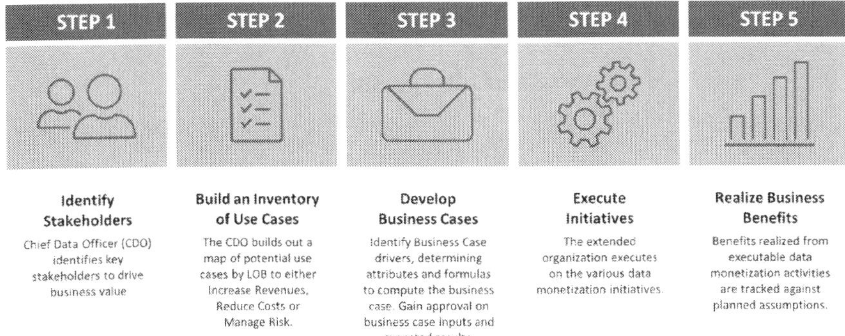

Figure 1.4: End-to-end approach to operationalize data monetization

The five steps to data monetization are explained below.

1. Identify Stakeholders

Data monetization relies on the engagement of key stakeholders. Stakeholders representing business and IT across the business can provide insights into the organization's strengths, weaknesses, and opportunities. Effective engagement with these stakeholders helps translate their needs into organizational goals and fosters contribution on many levels to carry out an effective strategy for data monetization. It is best to seek support at the outset from an executive leader such as the chief data officer.

With support from an executive leader, the next step is to determine the different types of stakeholders needed. This task depends on the information to be gathered and on the expected responsibilities of each stakeholder during the identification, development, and execution of data monetization business cases.

The first stakeholders to engage should include senior leaders who, through initial interviews, can provide key organizational strategic objectives, goals, and challenges, such as growing revenues, reducing costs, and managing risks. Next, business stakeholders representing specific lines of business tied to corporate goals and objectives should be identified. These business stakeholders are generally business leaders who have a deep understanding of key operational and strategic business drivers that can influence monetization initiatives. Interactions with business stakeholders include interviews, workshops, and ongoing interactions throughout an initiative to assist in developing and confirming business case assumptions and in reviewing and validating findings and realized benefits.

2. Build an Inventory of Use Cases

The next step is to translate business imperatives or initiatives into an inventory of tangible monetization opportunities or use cases. Structured interview methods should be utilized to extract and gather insights and direction from stakeholders. An effective way of doing this is to hold a white-board session using a strengths, weaknesses, opportunities, and threats (SWOT) approach. After interviewing stakeholders, the foundation for primary data monetization themes and their associated value should emerge.

Nearly all themes can be tied to internal data for which potential data monetization use cases can be developed. This can include use cases for areas such as regulatory reporting where there may be a concern with compliance, inhibitors to growing revenues through cross/up-selling, or the need for improved client retention by enhancing the customer experience.

The inventory of use cases should be evaluated and prioritized based on their potential realization of monetary value and feasibility in execution. The ability to execute should be based on existing capabilities and an estimation of the required cross-functional disciplines of enterprise data management, technology, legal engineering, and finance.

3. Develop Business Cases

The next step is to build an inventory of use cases that can be used to target the data monetization projects. Each business case will analyze the potential fulfillment of the strategic monetization initiative. These inventories can be developed along the different divisions and the operational lines of business within the organization. To assist in this, additional individuals with closer subject matter expertise (SME) and clear insight into the drivers of the use case should be identified. This team of core SMEs will be able to provide more-specific information and direction, validate findings, and make recommendations for developing each business case. They should also remain active through the execution of the initiative.

Each business case should substantiate one of the initial use cases for data monetization. The purpose of developing the business case is to demonstrate the financial benefits and value the initiative will provide. This is done by evaluating the impact of the current state data issues on an initiative and deriving an estimated financial return based on quantifying actions taken to address those issues and assumptions used.

The core SMEs/stakeholders will help identify and quantify the current state deficiencies and the root-cause critical data elements and activities and will help build the model to support the forecasted financial outcome assimilated from addressing current state limitations.

4. Execute Initiatives

Once business cases have been built, reviewed, and validated, stakeholders are ready to execute on the actual monetization initiatives. Depending on the initiative and the critical data drivers, various data management activities will be initiated. For example, data quality issues identified as a key component of the business case will need to be remediated. This task involves ensuring business rules are implemented through data quality rules that can be applied to critical data elements and tracked. It may involve establishing stewardship responsibilities and creating workflows to assign, execute, and update data issues.

Roles involved in executing initiatives will vary depending on the business case. However, core participants include data owners, data stewards, and business, financial, quality, and technical analysts, as well as enterprise and line-of-business governance advisors. A responsibility assignment (RACI) matrix is recommended.

As each initiative in a business case is executed, assumptions used in computing financial gains will need to be assessed, validated, and perhaps adjusted so that expectations are kept in check. Most important, results need to be tracked to show progress.

5. Realize Business Benefits

The final step to operationalizing data monetization is to realize the business benefits of each initiative. Every actionable component of a business case will involve certain tasks that need to be carried out by those identified in the business case RACI. The monetary impact or outcomes will be tracked against assumptions. As actions are taken and results are realized, the business case is updated.

The "potential" realizable monetary outcomes related to data management tasks undertaken (e.g., costs reduced, revenue generated) may need to be validated or certified before being recorded in the business case as "actual" or "realized."

Data monetization dashboards can be used to track the progress for each business case and provide summaries by line of business and monetization initiative. Dashboards will help keep stakeholders on all levels up-to-date and engaged in data monetization efforts.

Summary

EDM programs have lacked business adoption due to a limited tie-in with financial benefits. Data monetization is a cross-functional discipline that draws from best practices in enterprise data management, technology, legal engineering, and finance to leverage data to increase revenues, reduce costs, and manage risk.

2

Identify Stakeholders

The first step in the journey is to identify stakeholders to leverage and monetize data in alignment with the organization's strategy. Stakeholders are chosen from each line of business (LOB) and division for which there is an initiative to drive business value. Stakeholders should represent both the business and IT and will drive not only business cases but also tracking of data monetization efforts.

Identify Lines of Business

The organization should be decomposed into the LOBs and divisions that are most likely to generate value from data monetization efforts. For example, a financial services firm consists of retail banking, commercial banking, investment management, investment banking, treasury, risk management, finance, human resources, enterprise data and analytics, and information technology LOBs.

Identify Divisions or Departments

The LOBs may contain one or more divisions or departments. For example, the retail banking LOB contains retail lending, deposits, customer service, marketing, and regulatory compliance (Figure 2.1).

Lines of Business in Financial Services	
Line of Business	Division
Retail Banking	Retail Lending
	Deposits
	Customer Service
	Marketing
	Regulatory Compliance
Commercial Banking	Commercial Lending
Investment Management	Asset Management
Investment Banking	Sales & Trading
Treasury	
Risk Management	Credit Risk
	Market Risk
	Operational Risk
	Liquidity Risk
Finance	
Human Resources	
Enterprise Data & Analytics	Enterprise Data Management
	Data Analytics
Information Technology	Application Development

Figure 2.1: Lines of business and divisions in financial services

Summary

The first step in data monetization is to identify stakeholders that will drive business benefits. These stakeholders are chosen from each LOB and division for which there is an initiative to drive business value. This chapter provided a list of stakeholders in financial services.

3

Build Inventory of Use Cases

After stakeholders have been identified, the second step to monetizing data is to work with the stakeholders to begin translating business initiatives and imperatives into use cases. These use cases may be broadly categorized into increasing revenues, reducing costs, and managing risks.

Identify Use Cases

Data monetization may be tied to the internal use of data for current business processes, as well as supporting process improvement initiatives and managing risk and compliance. It can also be realized externally by directly sharing or selling data with third parties.

Within each line of business and division, data monetization may support an inventory of use cases (initiatives) to address business issues and opportunities to increase revenues, reduce costs, and manage risk (Figure 3.1).

1. Increase Revenues
2. Reduce Costs
3. Manage Risks

Figure 3.1: Business outcomes of data monetization

Figure 3.2 shows a summary of use cases by stakeholder at a typical financial services firm. Each use case is tied to a line of business, division, and use case type. For example, the *Reduce dropout rate associated with customers not being able to buy additional products due to incorrect dates of birth* use case is of the *Increase Revenues* use case type within the *Retail Lending* division, which is part of the *Retail Banking* line of business. This use case will be analyzed in more detail in subsequent chapters.

Line of Business	Division	Use Case Type	Use Case
Retail Banking	Retail Lending 1	Increase Revenues	· Reduce dropout rate associated with customers not being able to buy additional products due to incorrect dates of birth
	Customer Service 2	Reduce Costs	· Reduce the number and duration of customer service calls by improving customer data quality
	Marketing 1	Increase Revenues	· Increase sales by improving the number of products per customer through a cross-sell program based on Customer Master Data Management
	Regulatory Compliance 3	Manage Risk	· Home Mortgage Disclosure Act (HMDA) · Bank Secrecy Act/Anti Money Laundering (BSA/AML)
Information Technology	Information Security 3	Manage Risk	· Improve application security by certifying application ownership
	Application Development 2	Reduce Costs	· Retire applications not being used
Chief Data Office	Analytics 2	Reduce Costs	· Retire reports not being used
	Data Management 1	Increase Revenues	· Share or sell data externally
	Data Management 3	Manage Risk	· Share data internally

Figure 3.2: Inventory of data monetization use cases in financial services

The next three sections provide an overview of financial services use cases to increase revenues, reduce costs, and manage risks.

Sample Use Case to Increase Revenues

The marketing division in a financial services firm wants to increase sales by growing the number of products per customer. The firm has fragmented customer records across retail lending, credit cards, and deposits. By implementing a master data management program, the marketing department is able to pinpoint the fact that John Smith has a checking account but no credit cards or mortgages with the institution. The marketing department then institutes a sales campaign to reach out to customers such as John Smith and make compelling offers to buy additional products.

Sample Use Case to Reduce Costs

Information Asset's Data Governance in a Box approach introduces a 16-step process to identify critical data elements (CDEs) and critical data sets.[6] However, a lack of understanding of what constitutes a CDE may result in over-identification of CDEs, which can be expensive in terms of effort and resources.

As a rule of thumb, CDEs should not constitute more than 10 to 15 percent of an organization's data elements. Consider an application that may have 1,000 data elements, of which 50 may be deemed critical.

Table 3.1 provides the number of estimated hours a steward spends initially setting up 50 CDEs in accordance with an organization's policies and standards, as well as the consistent monthly maintenance of the CDEs.

Applying an average salary[7] to the estimated hours, the average organization may spend more than $159,567 to set up 50 CDEs in one application and more than $382,962 to maintain these same CDEs in one application for one year. While these numbers may look rather small at first glance, consider the average number of applications an organization owns, and then multiply that by these figures. This analysis indicates why it is important for data governance teams to constrain the number of CDEs.

---

[6] Sunil Soares, *Data Governance Guide for BCBS 239 and DFAST Compliance*, Information Asset, LLC, 2016

[7] Indeed.com, "How much does a Business Analyst make in the United States?" https://www.indeed.com/career/business-analyst/salaries

Table 3.1: Estimated stewardship efforts for CDE		
Functions	**CDE initial setup (hours)**	**CDE maintenance (hours/month)**
General setup	50	10
Stewardship	175	35
Governance	400	80
Architecture	250	50
Metadata management	250	50
Data quality management	700	140
Data delivery lifecycle	325	65
Information lifecycle	600	120
Sensitive data management	1,400	280
Total	*4,150*	*830*

Sample Use Case to Manage Risk

Another use case is managing the risk associated with potential non-compliance with the Home Mortgage Disclosure Act (HMDA) within the regulatory compliance division of a retail bank. This use case is based on the ability to legally engineer the necessary data anonymization policies for loan-level mortgage data. This reduces the risk that the personal data of loan applicants and borrowers is publicly exposed in HMDA compliance reports to the regulators.

Use Case Inventory Template

A template such as the one provided in Figure 3.3 may be used to record and track the status of data monetization use cases. Each use case in the summary list should be substantiated further to enable broader understanding across stakeholders who may be directly or indirectly impacted.

Linking and Prioritizing Use Cases to Strategic Objectives

The linking of use cases to organizational and corporate strategic objectives helps garner support and alignment with senior managers and executives. It also establishes the premise on which the execution of data-driven initiatives will generate financial value as identified in each supplementary business case.

Many use cases can be enacted simultaneously, but it is a good idea to socialize them with both senior leaders and subject matter experts closer to the initiatives to assess execution priorities. Business impact should be evaluated along with the level of effort and feasibility in implementation in terms of availability of resources and technology constraints.

Template for Use Case Inventory
Use Case Name: One-sentence description of the use case
Overview: One to two sentences providing a high-level summary of the initiative and its primary objective
Use Case Type: (Increase Revenues, Decrease Costs, Manage Risks)
Link to Organizational Strategic Objective: Description of how the use case ties back to one or more of the organization's key strategies. (e.g. 2021 Focus - Growing Customer Share of Wallet)
Use Case Owner: Name of the LOB / Division Stakeholder who is accountable and oversees the implementation and execution of the initiative
Use Case Coordinator(s): Names of the LOB / Division Stakeholders who are responsible for developing the business case, executing the initiative and tracking results. Stakeholders should represent both the business and IT.
Priority: (High, Medium, Low) Based on estimated level of effort and return on investment (very high-level analysis)
Status: Status of the submitted use case (In Review, Approved, In Progress, Completed)
Start Date: Effective date the initiative was executed
End Date: Effective date the initiative ended

Figure 3.3: Use case inventory template

Summary

The second step in data monetization is for the stakeholders identified in step one to build an inventory of use cases based on opportunities to capitalize business opportunities and to drive strategic initiatives. Use cases should be prioritized based on the level of effort and anticipated return on investment. Ensuring that the inventory is current with a pipeline of further data monetization opportunities will keep data management and governance activities front and center and will foster stronger business adoption and stakeholder alignment.

4

Develop Business Cases

The next step in the journey is to build a business case for each data monetization use case.

Start with Use Case

In this case, a retail bank was looking to increase cross-sell opportunities to their existing customers. However, they found that these cross-sell opportunities were hampered due to poor data quality. For example, a customer would call the bank requesting a new product. As part of the account verification process, customer service found that the customer's date of birth did not match the bank's internal records. Customer service would then suspend the new product sale and ask the customer to visit a branch and present proof of identity in the form of a passport or other document. In a significant portion of cases, such customers would drop out of the product sale process and go to the bank's competition, resulting in lost revenues and operating margin for the bank.

Identify Business Case Drivers

The next step is to identify the drivers of the business case. These business case drivers are typically CDEs—the 10 to 15 percent of data that is important to a business outcome.

The drivers for the *Reduce dropout rate* business case are *Date of Birth*, *Customer*, *Dropout Rate*, and *Operating Margin* (Figure 4.1). Each driver is a CDE and needs to have a clear, concise definition.

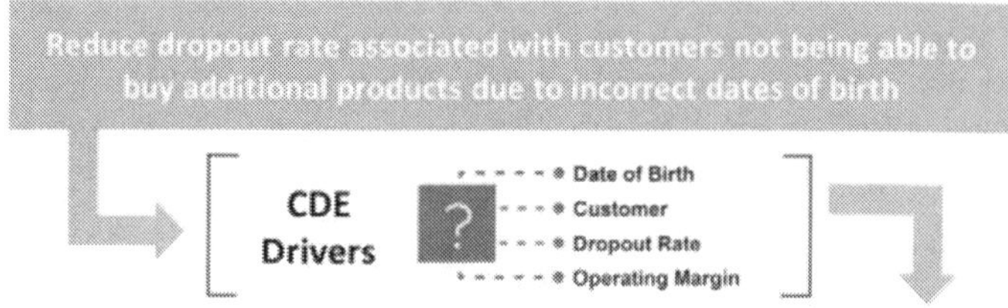

Figure 4.1: Business case drivers for reducing dropout rate associated with customers unable to buy additional products due to incorrect dates of birth

Compute Estimated Financial Benefits

The next step is to compute the estimated financial benefits. This exercise is usually iterative and is developed jointly with finance and the business. As shown in Figure 4.2, the bank started with 10 million customers, of whom 5 percent were estimated to have inaccurate dates of birth. Of the 500,000 customers with inaccurate dates of birth, 10 percent (or 50,000) called the bank each year with a request to buy another product, and 50 percent of those dropped out. The bank estimated that it lost 25,000 cross-sell opportunities each year due to poor date-of-birth quality. After applying the average value of a product sale of $20,000 and average operating margin of 5 percent, the bank estimated that it could increase annual operating margin by $25M by improving date-of-birth quality.

Business Case: Improve Date of Birth Quality to Grow Revenues	
A. Number of customers in the retail bank	10,000,000
B. Estimated percentage of customer records with inaccurate dates of birth	5%
C. Estimated number of retail banking customers with inaccurate dates of birth (A x B)	500,000
D. Annual percentage of customers who call the bank with a request to buy another product	10%
E. Average dropout rate associated with customers who have to visit a branch to correct inaccurate dates of birth before the bank can sell them an additional product	50%
F. Estimated number of annual cross-sell opportunities that are lost because of dropouts from inaccurate dates of birth (C x D x E)	25,000
G. Average value of product that is cross-sold to existing customers	$20,000
H. Average operating margin on products that are cross-sold to existing customers	5%
I. Potential increase in annual operating margin by improving the quality of dates of birth for existing retail banking customers (F x G x H)	**$25,000,000**

Figure 4.2: Estimated financial benefits from improving the quality of date of birth at a retail bank

Data Monetization Dashboard

YourDataConnect™ is a software-as-a-service (SaaS) platform for executing data monetization initiatives. Within the platform, initiatives are referred to as business cases, are grouped by line of business, and are sub-grouped into one of three objectives:

- Grow revenues
- Reduce costs
- Mitigate risks

A data monetization dashboard in YourDataConnect shows a summary of all business cases that have been defined in YourDataConnect. Figure 4.3 shows the initial state of this dashboard with zero dollars in the estimated value of business cases. The dashboard will be updated as new business cases are defined.

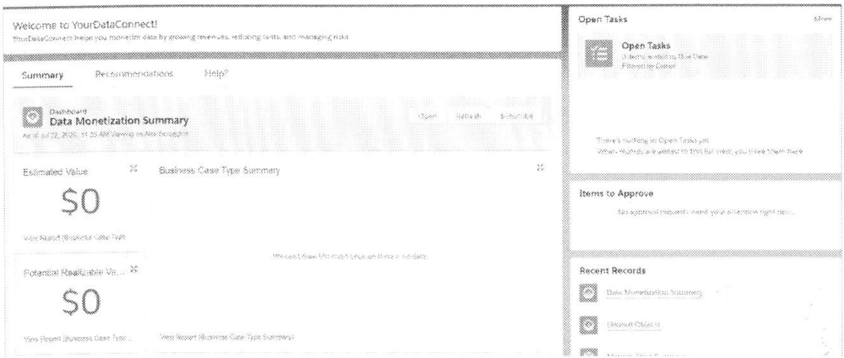

Figure 4.3: YourDataConnect™ data monetization dashboard shows zero dollars in estimated value of business cases

Estimated Value refers to an estimate calculated by YourDataConnect for each business case. *Potential Realizable Value* is calculated for a business case as actions are taken in response to the business case. For example, for a business case around retiring unused business intelligence reports, *Potential Realizable Value* will be updated to reflect the potential cost savings of retiring reports; it is a rolling sum that will increment as more and more reports are retired.

Figure 4.4 shows an empty business case form. All business cases require a name, sponsor, industry, line of business, and type to be selected.

Figure 4.4: Business case form in YourDataConnect

After entering the preliminary fields, the user populates a series of contextual fields based on the specific type of business case. Figure 4.5 shows the inputs required for the *Improve DOB Data Quality to Increase Up/Cross-Sell Opportunities* business case.

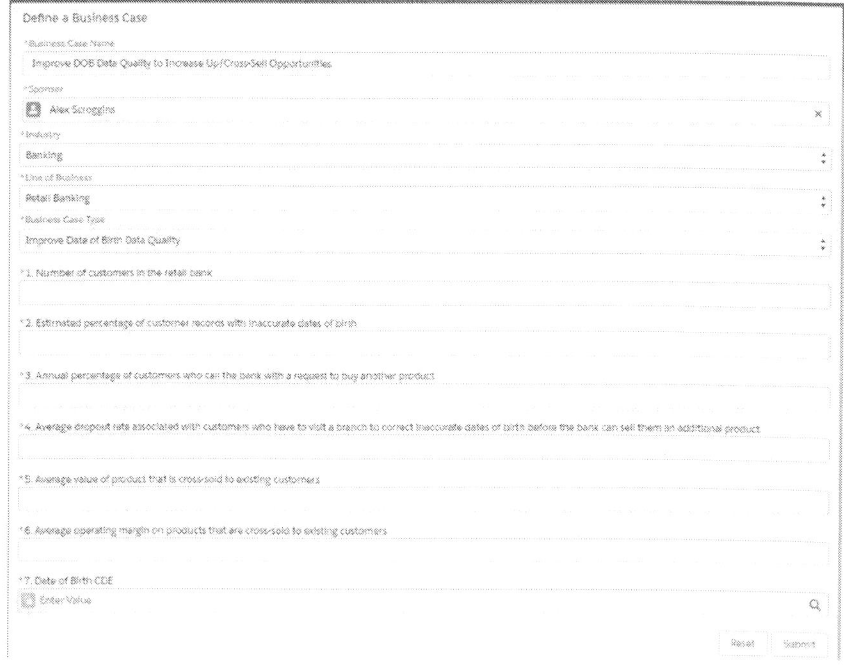

Figure 4.5: Business case input form for Improve DOB Data Quality to Increase Up/Cross-Sell Opportunities

The contextual questions are configurable and allow users to enter any variable relevant to the business case. Figure 4.6 shows the user providing a variety of types of inputs related to *Improve DOB Data Quality to Increase Up/Cross-Sell Opportunities*.

Define a Business Case

* Business Case Name
Improve DOB Data Quality to Increase Up/Cross-Sell Opportunities

* Sponsor
Alex Scroggins

* Industry
Banking

* Line of Business
Retail Banking

* Business Case Type
Improve Date of Birth Data Quality

* 1. Number of customers in the retail bank
10,000,000

* 2. Estimated percentage of customer records with inaccurate dates of birth
5.00%

* 3. Annual percentage of customers who call the bank with a request to buy another product
10.00%

* 4. Average dropout rate associated with customers who have to visit a branch to correct inaccurate dates of birth before the bank can sell them an additional product
50.00%

* 5. Average value of product that is cross-sold to existing customers
$20,000.00

* 6. Average operating margin on products that are cross-sold to existing customers
5.00%

* 7. Date of Birth CDE
customer date of

Figure 4.6: User provides input into the business case for Improve DOB Data Quality to Increase Up/Cross-Sell Opportunities

After submitting the information in Figure 4.6, YourDataConnect calculates an estimated value for the business case. As shown in Figure 4.7, the estimated value of this business case is $25,000,000.

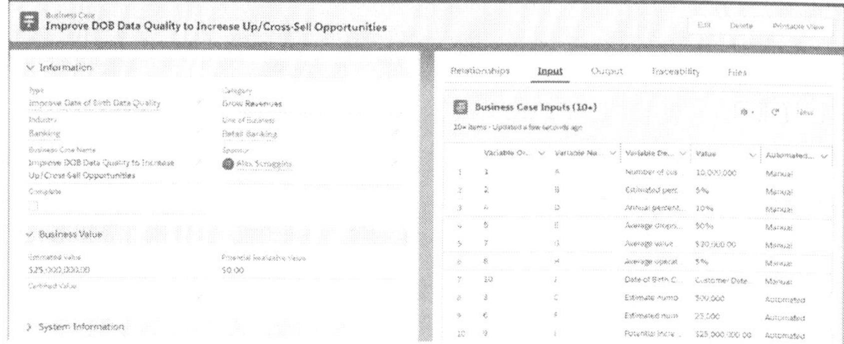

Figure 4.7: YourDataConnect computes the business case value

Submitting the business case also triggers an update to the estimated value in the YourDataConnect data monetization dashboard in Figure 4.8.

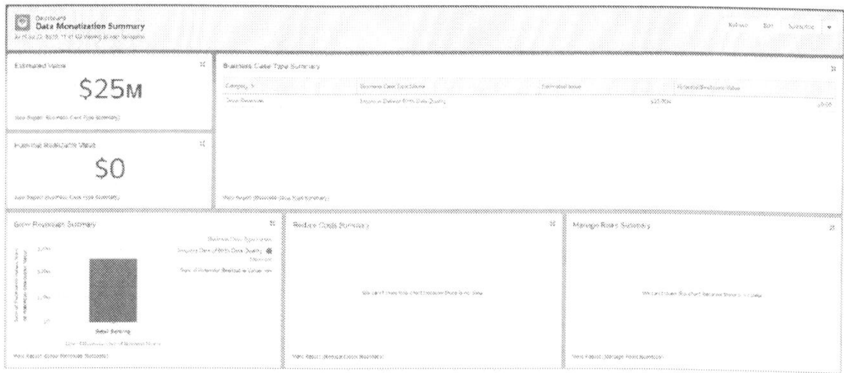

Figure 4.8: Estimated value of business case is updated in the YourDataConnect data monetization dashboard

Summary

The business case starts with identifying the drivers. The business case drivers are CDEs, which typically account for 10 to 15 percent of the data that is important to a business outcome. The financial benefits of the business case are then quantified. Finally, the estimated value of the business case is represented in the data monetization dashboard.

5

Execute Initiatives

The next step in the journey is to executive initiatives to actually monetize the data. This chapter will continue illustrating the *Improve DOB Data Quality to Increase Up/Cross-Sell Opportunities* business case. Obviously, there are additional mechanisms to monetize data beyond data quality, including master data management, sharing data, selling data, and cybersecurity.

Define Business Rules

To recap, the user selected a CDE named *Customer Date of Birth* when creating the business case. YourDataConnect™ also supports the creation of a business rule, such as *Customer DOB must be a past date and not null*, that can define validation logic for CDEs, as shown in Figure 5.1.

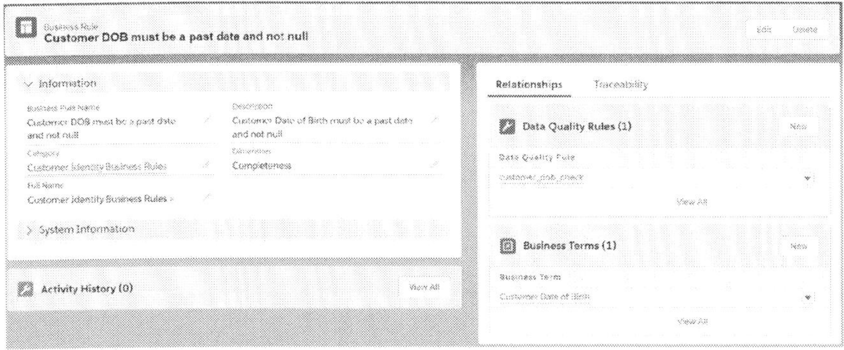

Figure 5.1: Business rule for Customer Date of Birth in YourDataConnect™

Implement Business Rules in Data Quality Tool

After business rules are approved in YourDataConnect, a workflow ensures they are physically implemented in a third-party data quality tool, such as Informatica® Data Quality or IBM® InfoSphere® Information Analyzer. Figure 5.2 shows the date-of-birth data quality rule implemented in IBM InfoSphere Information Analyzer.

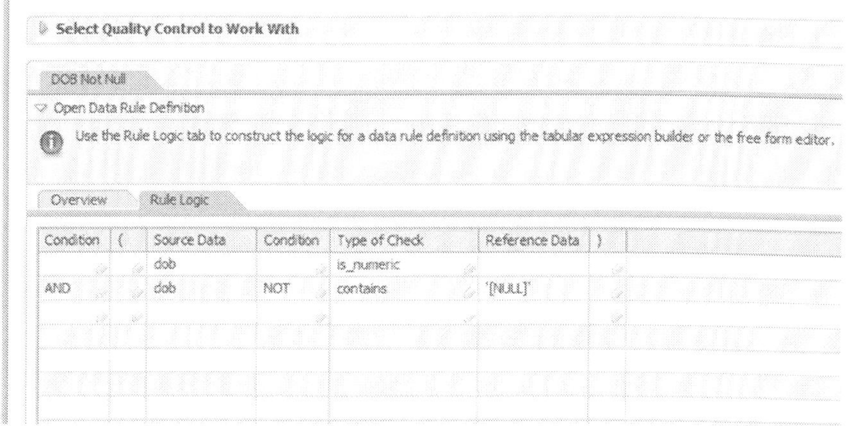

Figure 5.2: Date-of-birth data quality rule implemented in IBM® InfoSphere® Information Analyzer

The data quality tool executes the rule on a periodic basis to ascertain whether the customer date-of-birth data is valid per the rule. After the rule executes, metrics such as the number of valid rows and the number of invalid rows are captured by IBM InfoSphere Information Analyzer.

Assess and Remediate Data

YourDataConnect supports integrations with third-party data quality tools. After ingesting data quality metrics from IBM InfoSphere Information Analyzer, YourDataConnect sends a notification to users that 500,000 records need to be remediated out of a total of 10,500,000, which indicates 95.24 percent validity (Figure 5.3).

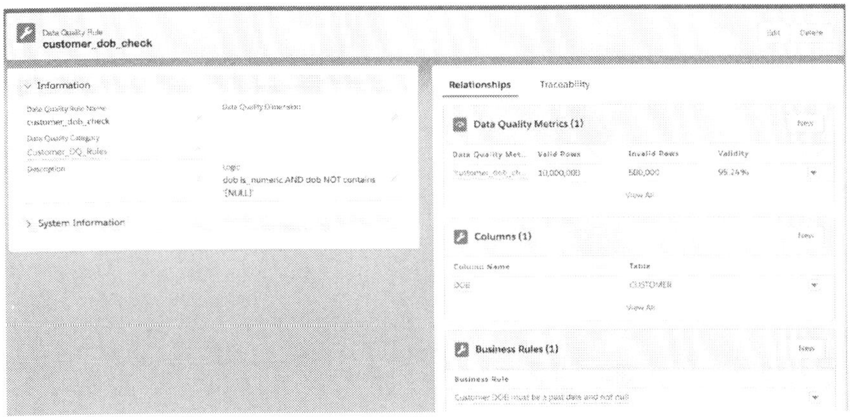

Figure 5.3: Data quality metrics ingested from IBM InfoSphere Information Analyzer into YourDataConnect

YourDataConnect automatically generates a data remediation task, which is assigned to the data owner (Figure 5.4).

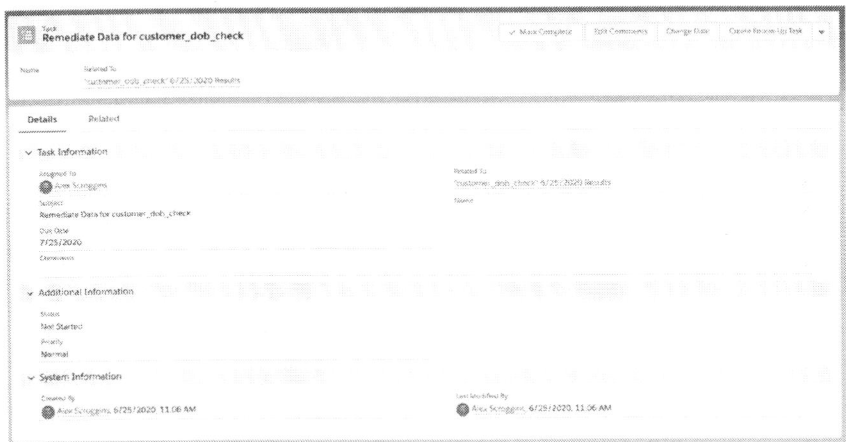

Figure 5.4: Data remediation task assigned to data owner in YourDataConnect

In Figure 5.5, the user has marked 100,000 rows as remediated in YourDataConnect.

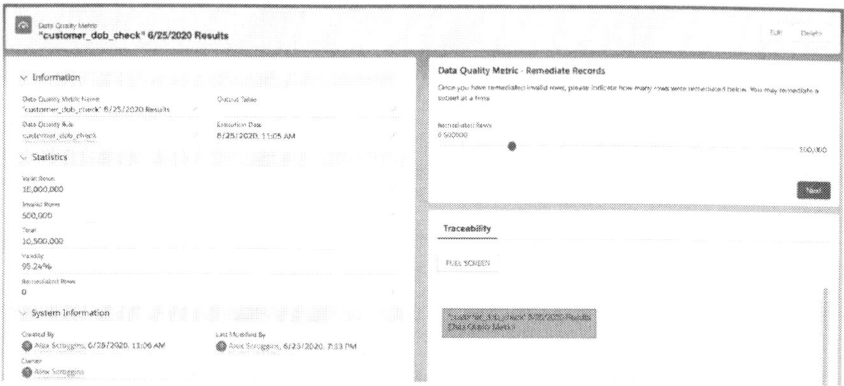

Figure 5.5: The user marked 100,000 rows as remediated in YourDataConnect

This triggers an update of $5,000,00 to the potential realizable value on the business case based on the initial estimated value of $50 per date-of-birth record (Figure 5.6).

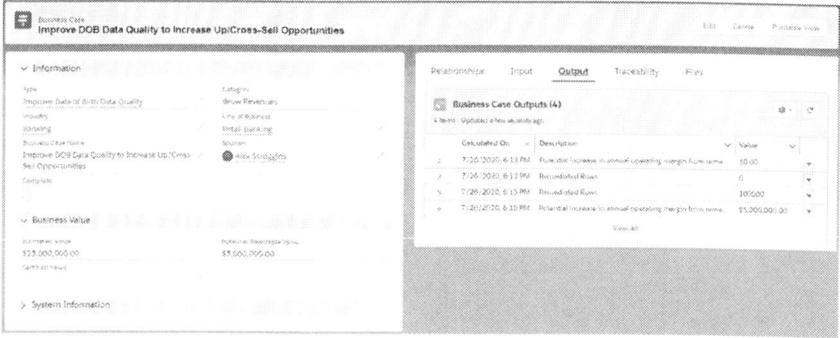

Figure 5.6: Potential realizable value updated to $5,000,000 in YourDataConnect based on remediation of date-of-birth records

The user then returns to the data quality metric and remediates the remaining 400,000 rows (Figure 5.7).

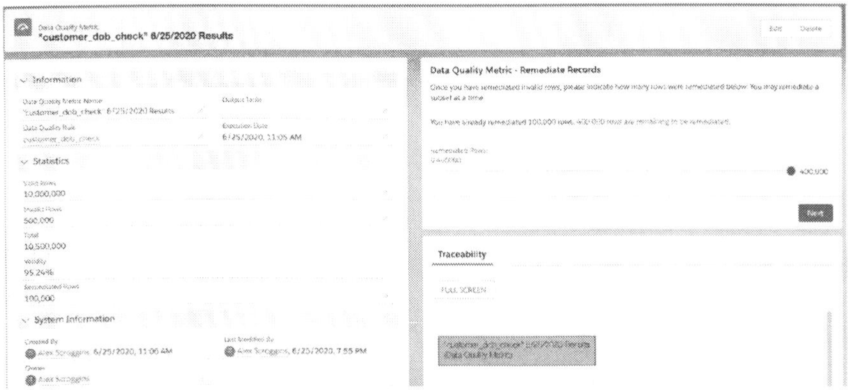

Figure 5.7: The user marks the remaining 400,000 rows as remediated in YourDataConnect

Remediating the remaining 400,000 rows increments the business case potential realizable value to $25,000,000, as shown in Figure 5.8.

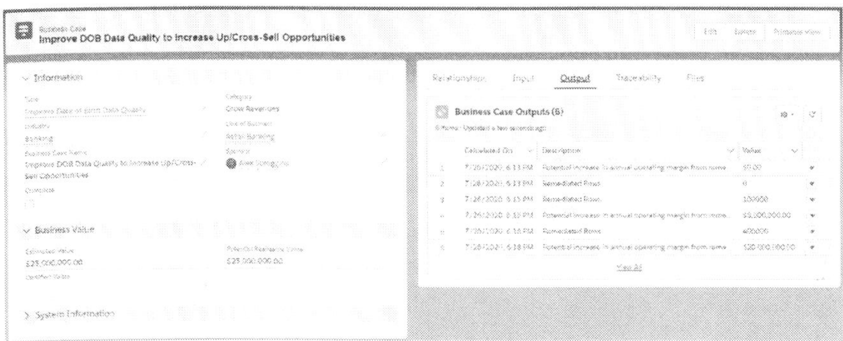

Figure 5.8: Potential realizable value of business case incremented to $25,000,000 in YourDataConnect

Summary

The next step in the journey is to executive initiatives to actually monetize the data. This chapter illustrated the *Improve DOB Data Quality to Increase Up/Cross-Sell Opportunities* business case. The chapter walked through a use case with IBM InfoSphere Information Analyzer and YourDataConnect to define business rules, capture data quality metrics, and remediate data.

6

Realize Business Benefits

The final step in the journey is to realize business benefits from data monetization.

Data Monetization Dashboard

The data monetization dashboard is a useful mechanism to present the business benefits to executive management. As Figure 6.1 depicts, the data monetization dashboard for a large financial institution shows the actual and cumulative benefits across four initiatives. These initiatives are spread across two lines of business and four divisions.

Data Monetization Dashboard for a Large Financial Institution

Line of Business	Division	Use Case Type	Use Case	Anticipated Benefits	Actual Benefits June 2020	Cumulative Benefits	
Retail Banking	Retail Lending	Increase Revenues	Improve Quality for Dates of Birth	$600,000	$40,000	$40,000	1
Retail Banking	Regulatory Compliance	Manage Risk	BSA/AML Compliance	$1,000,000	$100,000	$100,000	
Information Technology	Information Security	Manage Risk	Improve application security by certifying application ownership	$2,000,000	$150,000	$150,000	3
Information Technology	Application Development	Reduce Costs	Retire applications not being used	$100,000	$100,000	$100,000	2

Figure 6.1: Data monetization dashboard for large financial institution

As business cases are updated, the updates are reflected in the data monetization dashboard (Figure 6.2).

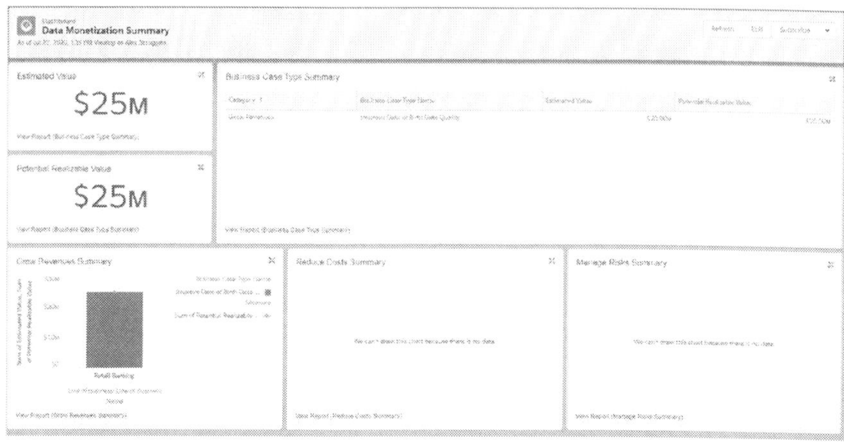

Figure 6.2: Updates to the business case are reflected in the data monetization dashboard in YourDataConnect™

Data Monetization Traceability

In addition, YourDataConnect™ provides traceability to allow users to explore all business and technical assets relevant to business cases from a single page in the platform. Reading Figure 6.3 from left to right, the summed monetary value of all business cases is shown first, then drilled down to line of business, then further drilled down to category (Grow Revenues, Reduce Costs, Manage Risks), and next drilled down to individual business cases. Individual business cases can be explored further to see the business terms, business rules, data quality rules, and additional data artifacts that are relevant to the business case.

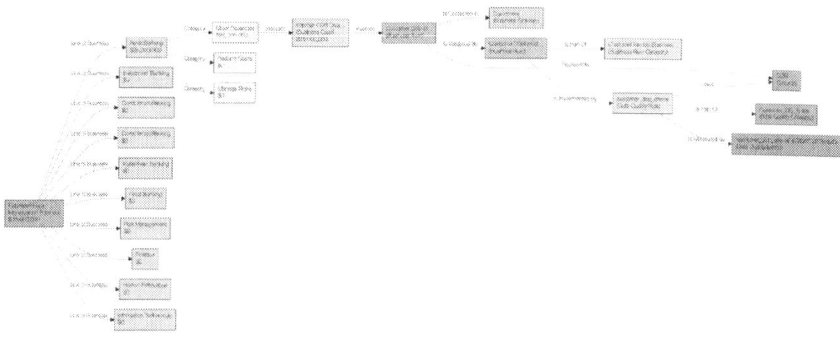

Figure 6.3: Data monetization traceability diagram in YourDataConnect

Summary

The final step in the journey is to realize business benefits from data monetization. The data monetization dashboard is a useful mechanism to present the business benefits to executive management. As business cases are updated, the updates are reflected in the data monetization dashboard in YourDataConnect. YourDataConnect also provides traceability to allow users to explore all business and technical assets relevant to business cases from a single page in the platform.

7

Legal Engineering

As was mentioned earlier, legal engineers use their legal knowledge combined with technological know-how and project management experience to optimize existing products, services, and processes and to create new solutions to specific problems faced by clients, using a combination of technology and tools.[8]

Legal engineering is a key component of data monetization to drive regulatory compliance. While there are many regulations, only a handful are data-intensive from a compliance perspective. These data-intensive regulations fall into several key categories (Figure 7.1):

- Sensitive data management
- Consumer protection laws
- Data-intensive industry regulations

---

[8] "The rise of the legal engineer," HighQ, part of Thomson Reuters, July 27, 2016, https://www.lexology.com/library/detail.aspx?g=f8d9bb92-3779-4bc2-9f1b-7354d416acb1#:~:text=Legal%20engineers%20use%20their%20legal,combination%20of%20technology%20and%20tools

Sensitive Data Management

California Consumer Privacy Act (CCPA), GDPR, Children's Online Privacy Protection Act (COPPA), Video Privacy Protection Act (VPPA

Consumer Protection

Community Reinvestment Act (CRA), Consumer Leasing Act (CLA), Electronic Fund Transfer Act (EFTA), Equal Credit Opportunity Act (ECOA), Fair Credit Reporting Act (FCRA), Fair Debt Collection Practices Act (FDCPA), Home Mortgage Disclosure Act (HMDA), Gramm-Leach-Bliley Act (GLBA), Truth in Lending Act (TILA), Real Estate Settlement Procedures Act (RESPA), Homeowners Protection Act (HPA), Secure and Fair Enforcement for Mortgage Licensing Act (SAFE Act), Truth in Savings Act (TISA), Unfair, Deceptive or Abusive Acts or Practices (UDAAPs)

Financial Services

Bank Secrecy Act/Anti-Money Laundering (BSA/AML), Comprehensive Capital Analysis and Review (CCAR), Current Expected Credit Loss (CECL), Dodd Frank Act Stress Test (DFAST), Office of Foreign Assets Control (OFAC), Financial Crimes Enforcement Network (FinCEN)

Life Sciences

Clinical Trials/Real-World Evidence, Identification of Medicinal Products (IDMP), European Union Medical Device Regulation (MDR)

Utilities

Smart Meter Data Governance & Privacy

Insurance

International Financial Reporting Standard 9 (IFRS 9), IFRS 17

Figure 7.1: Sample inventory of data-intensive regulations

The next few chapters will review these topics in detail.

Summary

Legal engineering is a key component of data monetization to drive regulatory compliance. While there are many regulations, only a handful are data-intensive from a compliance perspective.

8

Sensitive Data Management

Sensitive data management (SDM) harmonizes the relationship between people, processes, and technology to protect sensitive data.

Heightened Focus on Security and Privacy

In recent years, there has been significantly increasing focus by legislators, regulators, the public, and business leaders on privacy, data, information security, cybersecurity, and consumer protection due in part to a heightened risk and threat environment and new technologies. This has resulted in an evolving legal, regulatory, and contractual compliance landscape with new or enhanced laws, rules, regulations, and regulatory guidance at the U.S. state and federal levels, as well as internationally.

Sensitive Data

Sensitive data is any data that requires security standards to protect its confidentiality and integrity. These requirements may come from various sources, such as applicable laws, rules, regulations, and official regulatory guidance; self-regulatory frameworks; established industry standards; contractual requirements; or company-specific policies and standards. Sensitive data includes, but is not limited to, data related to customers, employees, and vendors, as well as intellectual property, trade secrets, and other confidential information.

European Union General Data Protection Regulation

The EU General Data Protection Regulation (GDPR), which took effect in 2018, provides increased requirements regarding the privacy and security of personal data of Europeans. The GDPR is increasingly regarded as a model for new or enhanced laws, rules, and regulations, even outside the EU.

Data monetization tooling needs to identify sensitive data. Figure 8.1 shows a *Personal Identifiable Information* glossary with business terms such as *Postal Address*, *Email Address*, *Driver's License Number*, *Passport Number*, and *Social Security Number* in YourDataConnect™.

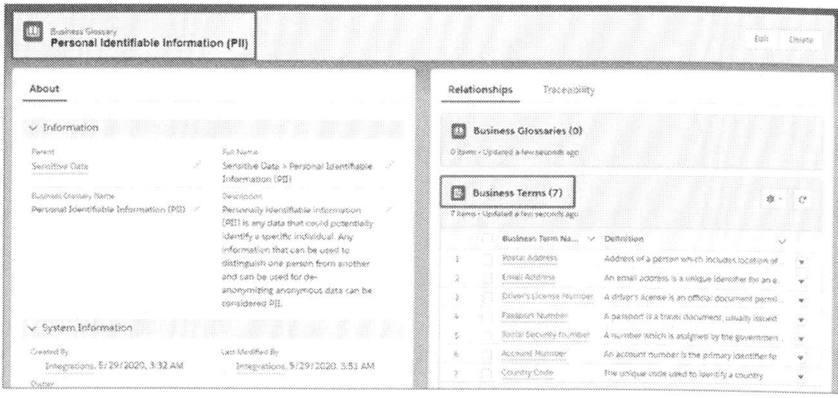

Figure 8.1: Personal identifiable information glossary in YourDataConnect™

Figure 8.2 shows a traceability diagram in YourDataConnect. The *Social Security Number* business term is contained in the *Personal Identifiable Information* business glossary, is validated by the *SSN completeness* business rule, and is regulated by the *California Consumer Privacy Act* regulation. The *Personal Identifiable Information* business glossary is a child of the *Sensitive Data* business glossary. The *SSN completeness* business rule is part of the *Sensitive Data Business Rules* category.

Finally, the CCPA regulation is associated with the *State of California* jurisdiction and the *Ensure that personal information is protected* policy.

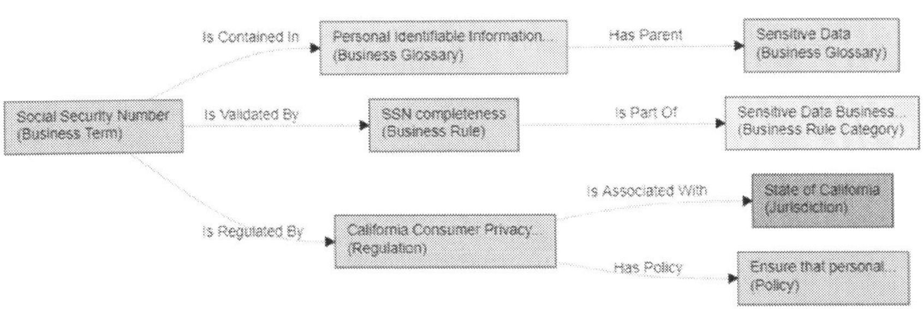

Figure 8.2: Traceability diagram in YourDataConnect

California Consumer Privacy Act

The California Consumer Privacy Act (CCPA) establishes rules that organizations must follow in order to process the personal data of California residents. Specifically, the CCPA gives California residents greater rights surrounding their data, including the right to be informed about what types of personal information covered companies have collected about them and whether or not that information has been shared with third parties.

Several data privacy regulations, such as the GDPR and the CCPA, allow data subjects to request access to their personal data subject to certain conditions. YourDataConnect provides workflow capability to support these Data Subject Access Requests (DSARs).

As a first step in the workflow, the data subject raises a *New Access Request Task* on the public portal hosted by YourDataConnect (Figure 8.3).

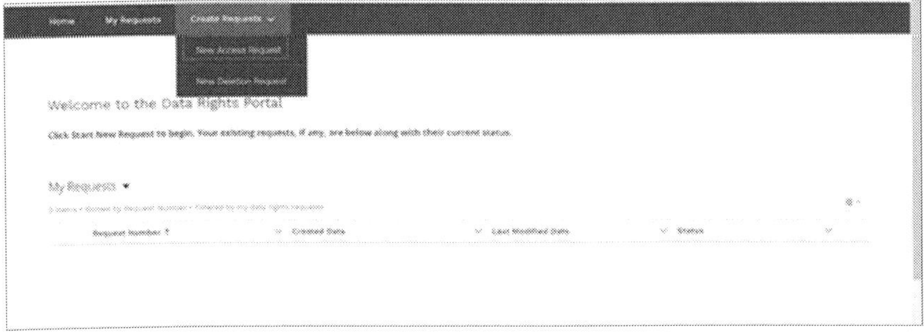

Figure 8.3: Data subject creates a New Access Request in YourDataConnect

A new *Data Rights Request* has been automatically created in YourDataConnect with *Pending* status (Figure 8.4).

Figure 8.4: Data Rights Request in Pending status in YourDataConnect

The data subject has their personal data stored in multiple systems, each with their own data owner. The *Data Rights Request* is now subdivided into a list of tasks assigned to each *Data Source Owner* (Figure 8.5).

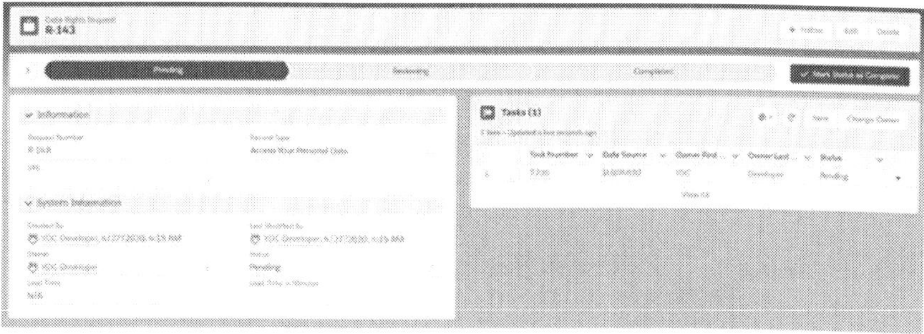

Figure 8.5: Data Rights Request is subdivided into individual tasks for each Data Source Owner in YourDataConnect

Each data source owner receives email notifications about their respective tasks. Each data source owner works on their assigned task and updates the status to *Completed* (Figure 8.6).

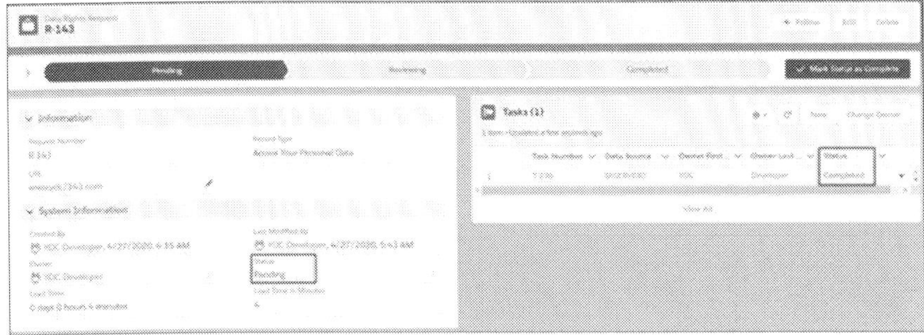

Figure 8.6: Data Rights Request with updated status for each task by data source owner

The DSAR administrator receives an email notification that all data source owner tasks have been completed. The DSAR administrator verifies the secure URL for the personal data and changes the status of the *Data Rights Request* to *Completed* (Figure 8.7).

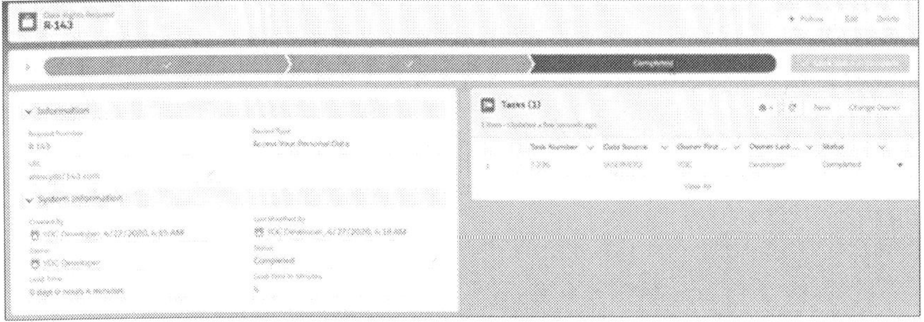

Figure 8.7: Status of Data Rights Request updated to Completed

The data subject receives an email notification with a secure URL where they can download their personal data (Figure 8.8).

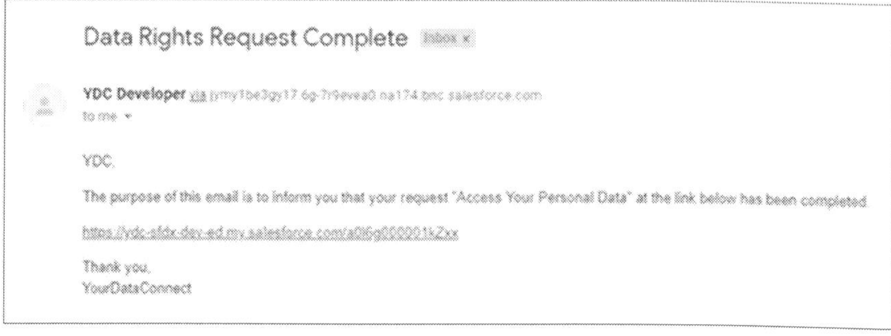

Figure 8.8: Email notification to data subject with secure URL

Children's Online Privacy Protection Act

The Children's Online Privacy Protection Act of 1998 (COPPA) is a United States federal law enacted on October 21, 1998. The act, effective April 21, 2000, applies to the online collection of personal information by persons or entities under U.S. jurisdiction about children under 13 years of age, including children outside the United States if the company is U.S. based. It details what a website operator must include in a privacy policy, when and how to seek verifiable consent from a parent or guardian, and what responsibilities an operator has to protect children's privacy and safety online, including restrictions on marketing to those under 13.[9]

While children under 13 can legally give out personal information with their parents' permission, many websites—particularly social media sites, but also other sites that collect most personal information—disallow children under 13 from using their services altogether due to the cost and work involved in complying with the law.

Video Privacy Protection Act

The Video Privacy Protection Act of 1988 was passed in reaction to the disclosure of Supreme Court nominee Robert Bork's video rental records in a newspaper. The act is not invoked often, but it stands as one of the strongest protections of consumer privacy against a specific form of data

---

[9] Wikipedia, "Children's Online Privacy Protection Act," https://en.wikipedia.org/wiki/Children%27s_Online_Privacy_Protection_Act

collection. Generally, it prevents disclosure of personally identifiable rental records of "prerecorded video cassette tapes or similar audio-visual material."[10]

Other Regulations

In addition to the aforementioned regulations, many other countries and jurisdictions have data privacy policies (see Table 8.1).

Table 8.1: Sample inventory of sensitive data management regulations

Jurisdiction	Regulation
Australia	Australian Privacy Act
California	California Consumer Privacy Act (CCPA)
Canada	Canada's Anti-Spam Legislation (CASL)
Canada	Personal Information Protection and Electronic Documents Act (PIPEDA)
China	People's Republic of China (PRC) Cybersecurity Law
European Union	General Data Protection Regulation (GDPR)
France	Data Protection Act (DPA)
Germany	Federal Data Protection Act
Hong Kong	Personal Data Privacy Ordinance
Ireland	Data Protection Acts of 1998 and 2003
Malaysia	Personal Data Act 2010
Russia	Russian Federal Law 152-FZ
Singapore	Personal Data Protection Act (PDPA)
United States	Children's Online Privacy Protection Act (COPPA)
United States	Video Privacy Protection Act (VPPA)

Summary

SDM harmonizes the relationship between people, processes, and technology to protect sensitive data. In recent years, there has been significantly increasing focus by legislators, regulators, the public, and business leaders on privacy, data, information security, cybersecurity, and consumer protection due in part to a heightened risk and threat

---

[10] Electronic Privacy Information Center, "Video Privacy Protection Act," https://epic.org/privacy/vppa

environment and new technologies. Sensitive data is any data that requires security standards to protect its confidentiality and integrity. GDPR, CCPA, COPPA, and VPPA are just a handful of the myriad sensitive data management regulations across the world. YourDataConnect allows companies to manage sensitive data and support DSAR requests.

9

Consumer Protection Law

Consumer protection law or consumer law is an area of law that regulates private law relationships between individual consumers and the businesses that sell those goods and services. Consumer protection covers a wide range of topics, including but not necessarily limited to product liability, privacy rights, unfair business practices, fraud, misrepresentation, and other interactions between consumers and businesses.

In the United States, a variety of laws at both the federal and state levels regulate consumer affairs. U.S. federal consumer protection laws are mainly enforced by the Federal Trade Commission (FTC), the Consumer Financial Protection Bureau (CFPB), the Food and Drug Administration (FDA), and the Department of Justice. Also, the majority of states, such as California, have a Department of Consumer Affairs devoted to regulating certain industries and protecting consumers who use goods and services from those industries.[11]

The European Union Consumer Rights Directive gives consumers the same strong rights across the EU. It aligns and harmonizes national consumer rules, for example on the information consumers need to be given before they purchase something and their right to cancel online purchases, wherever they shop in the EU.[12]

Consumer Financial Protection Bureau

The Consumer Financial Protection Bureau is an agency of the United States federal government responsible for consumer protection in the financial sector. CFPB's jurisdiction includes banks, credit unions,

---

[11] Wikipedia, "Consumer protection," https://en.wikipedia.org/wiki/Consumer_protection

[12] European Commission, "Consumer rights directive," https://ec.europa.eu/info/law/law-topic/consumers/consumer-contract-law/consumer-rights-directive_en

securities firms, payday lenders, mortgage-servicing operations, foreclosure relief services, debt collectors, and other financial services companies operating in the United States. The CFPB's creation was authorized by the Dodd-Frank Wall Street Reform and Consumer Protection Act of 2010 in response to the global financial crisis . The CFPB has regulatory purview over many consumer protection laws in the United States.[13]

The CFPB has enforcement authority over a number of U.S. federal laws, including the following:

- Community Reinvestment Act (CRA)
- Consumer Leasing Act (CLA)
- Electronic Fund Transfer Act (EFTA)
- Equal Credit Opportunity Act (ECOA)
- Fair Credit Reporting Act (FCRA)
- Fair Debt Collection Practices Act (FDCPA)
- Gramm-Leach-Bliley Act (GLBA)
- Home Mortgage Disclosure Act (HMDA)
- Homeowners Protection Act (HPA)
- Real Estate Settlement Procedures Act (RESPA)
- Secure and Fair Enforcement for Mortgage Licensing Act (SAFE Act)
- Truth in Lending Act (TILA)
- Truth in Savings Act (TISA)
- Unfair, Deceptive or Abusive Acts or Practices (UDAAPs)

Community Reinvestment Act

The Community Reinvestment Act (CRA) is a U.S. federal law designed to encourage commercial banks and savings associations to help meet the needs of borrowers in all segments of their communities, including low- and moderate-income neighborhoods. Congress passed the act in 1977 to reduce discriminatory credit practices against low-income neighborhoods, a practice known as redlining.

The CRA instructs the appropriate federal financial supervisory agencies to encourage regulated financial institutions to help meet the credit needs

[13] Wikipedia, "Consumer Financial Protection Bureau," https://en.wikipedia.org/wiki/Consumer_Financial_Protection_Bureau

of the local communities in which they are chartered, consistent with safe and sound operation. To enforce the statute, federal regulatory agencies examine banking institutions for CRA compliance and take this information into consideration when approving applications for new bank branches or for mergers or acquisitions.

The law does not list specific criteria for evaluating the performance of financial institutions. Rather, it directs that the evaluation process should accommodate the situation and context of each individual institution. Federal regulations dictate agency conduct in evaluating a bank's compliance in five performance areas, comprising twelve assessment factors. This examination culminates in a rating and a written report that becomes part of the supervisory record for that bank.

The same banking agencies that are responsible for supervising depository institutions are also the agencies that conduct examinations for CRA compliance. These agencies are the Federal Reserve System (FRS), the Federal Deposit Insurance Corporation (FDIC), and the Office of the Comptroller of the Currency (OCC). In 1981, to help achieve the goals of the CRA, each of the Federal Reserve banks established a Community Affairs Office to work with banking institutions and the public in identifying credit needs within the community and ways to address those needs.

The Federal Financial Institutions Examination Council (FFIEC) coordinates inter-agency information about the CRA. Information about the CRA ratings of individual banking institutions from the three responsible agencies (Federal Reserve, FDIC, and OCC), is publicly available from the website of the FFIEC.

The CRA followed similar laws passed to reduce discrimination in the credit and housing markets, including the Fair Housing Act of 1968, the Equal Credit Opportunity Act of 1974, and the Home Mortgage Disclosure Act of 1975 (HMDA). The Fair Housing Act and the Equal Credit Opportunity Act prohibit discrimination on the basis of race, sex, or other personal characteristics. The Home Mortgage Disclosure Act requires that financial institutions publicly disclose mortgage lending and application data. In contrast with these acts, the CRA seeks to ensure the provision of credit to all parts of a community, regardless of the relative wealth or poverty of a neighborhood.[14]

---

[14] Wikipedia, "Community Reinvestment Act," https://en.wikipedia.org/wiki/Community_Reinvestment_Act

Table 9.1 shows sample CDEs for CRA compliance.[15]

Table 9.1: CDEs for CRA compliance

Critical data element	Definition
1. MSA Code	Next to each county in a Metropolitan Statistical Area (MSA) appears the number of the MSA, as announced by the Office of Management and Budget (OMB).
2. MD Code	Eleven MSAs having a single core with a population of 2.5 million or more (Boston, Chicago, Dallas, Detroit, Los Angeles, Miami, New York, Philadelphia, San Francisco, Seattle, and Washington) are subdivided into Metropolitan Divisions (MDs).
3. Census Tract	A small, relatively permanent statistical subdivision of a county in a metropolitan area or a selected nonmetropolitan county designed to be a relatively homogeneous unit with respect to population characteristics, economic status, and living conditions. Census tracts usually contain between 2,500 and 8,000 inhabitants.
4. Income	The gross annual income of the borrower that the institution considered in making its credit decision (consumer loans).
5. Loan Number	A unique identifier for the loan.

Figure 9.1 shows the CDEs for CRA in YourDataConnect™.

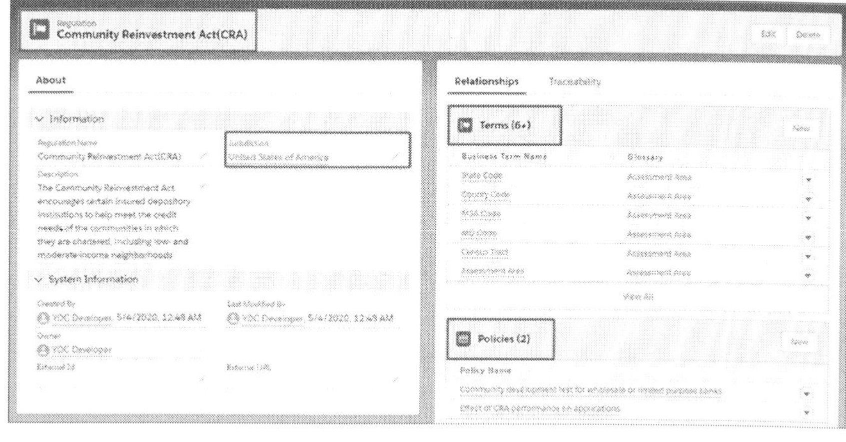

Figure 9.1: CRA CDEs in YourDataConnect™

[15] Federal Financial Institutions Examination Council, *A Guide to CRA Data Collection and Reporting*, https://www.ffiec.gov/cra/pdf/2013_CRA_Guide.pdf

Table 9.2 describes sample data quality rules for CRA.[16]

Table 9.2: Data quality rules for CRA compliance	
Critical data element	**Data quality rule**
1. Loan Type	Type of loan must equal one of the following: 01 = Small Business Loan 02 = Small Farm Loan 03 = Other Lines/Loans for Purposes of Small Business 04 = Home Equity 05 = Motor Vehicle 06 = Credit Card 07 = Other Secured Consumer Loans 08 = Other Unsecured Consumer Loans 09 = Other Loan Data
2. Loan Number	Loan number must not be null or blank and must be unique for a given loan type.
3. MSA/MD Number, State Code, County Code, Census Tract	Census tract must equal a valid census tract number for the MSA (or MD)/state/county combination, NA if the street address does not exist, *or* a valid census tract number for the state/county combination where MSA/MD = NA (outside a MSA/MD area).
4. Action Taken Type	Action taken type must equal Originated or Purchased.
5. Income (Consumer Loans)	If type of loan = 01, 02, or 03, then consumer loan income must equal 0000.
6. Income (Consumer Loans)	If type of loan = 04, 05, 06, 07, 08, or 09, then consumer loan income must be numeric and > 0.

[16] Federal Financial Institutions Examination Council, "2019 CRA Edits," https://www.ffiec.gov/cra/pdf/edit2019.pdf

Figure 9.2 shows the CRA data quality rules for *State Code* in YourDataConnect.

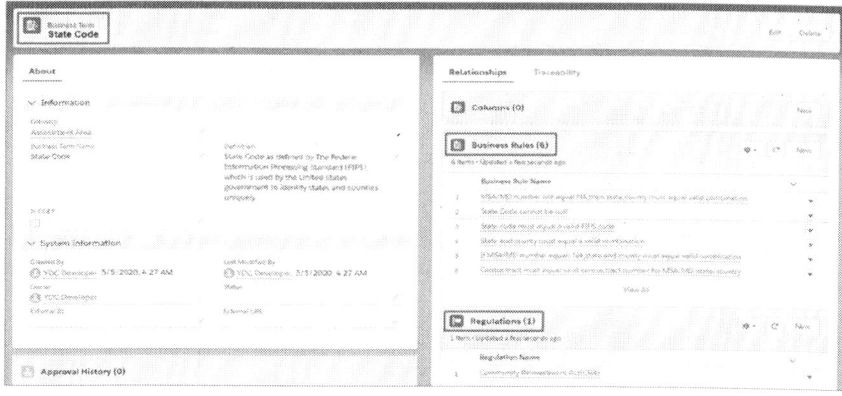

Figure 9.2: CRA data quality rules for State Code in YourDataConnect

Consumer Leasing Act

For consumers, leasing is an alternative to buying property either with cash or on credit. A lease is a contract between a lessor (the property owner) and a lessee (the property user) for the use of property subject to stated terms and limitations for a specified period and at a specified payment. The Consumer Leasing Act (CLA) was passed in 1976 to assure that meaningful and accurate disclosure of lease terms is provided to consumers before entering into a contract. It applies to consumer leases of personal property. With this information, consumers can more easily compare one lease with another, as well as compare the cost of leasing with the cost of buying on credit or the opportunity cost of paying cash. In addition, the CLA puts limits on balloon payments sometimes due at the end of a lease and regulates advertising. The CLA was originally part of the Truth in Lending Act and was implemented by Federal Reserve Regulation Z. When Regulation Z was revised in 1981, Regulation M was issued and contained those provisions that govern consumer leases. The Dodd-Frank Act granted enforcement and rulemaking authority under the CLA to the Consumer Financial Protection Bureau.[17]

---

[17] Consumer Financial Protection Bureau, "Consumer Leasing Act," https://files.consumerfinance.gov/f/documents/102012_cfpb_consumer-leasing-act_procedures.pdf

Table 9.3 reviews sample CDEs for CLA compliance.

Table 9.3: CDEs for CLA compliance	
Critical data element	**Definition**
1. Realized Value	Price received by the lessor of the leased property at disposition, the highest offer for disposition of the leased property, or the fair market value of the leased property at the end of the lease term.
2. Residual Value	Value of the leased property at the end of the lease, as estimated or assigned at consummation of the lease by the lessor.
3. Open-End Lease	Lease in which the amount owed at the end of the lease term is based on the difference between the residual value of the leased property and its realized value. (The consumer may pay all or part of the difference if the realized value is less than the residual value, or they may get a refund if the realized value is greater than the residual value at scheduled termination.)
4. Closed-End Lease	Lease other than an open-end lease, which allows the consumer to "walk away" at the end of the contract period, with no further payment obligation—unless the property has been damaged or has sustained abnormal wear and tear.

Figure 9.3 shows sample CDEs for CLA compliance in YourDataConnect.

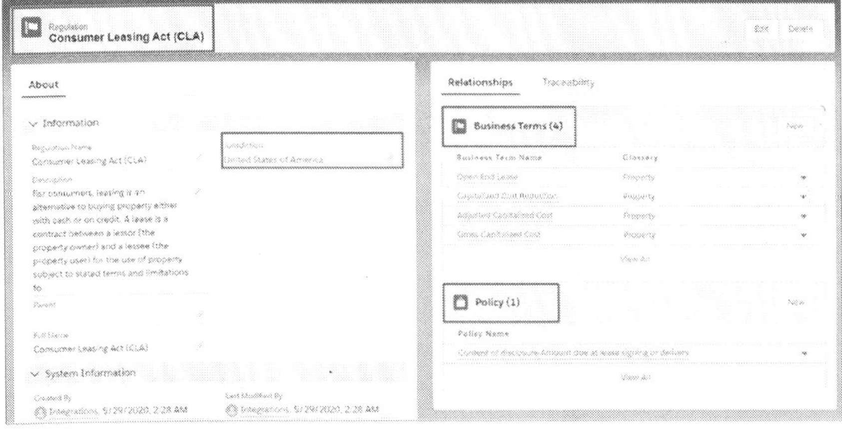

Figure 9.3: CLA CDEs in YourDataConnect

Electronic Fund Transfer Act

The Electronic Fund Transfer Act (EFTA) was passed by the U.S. Congress in 1978 to establish the rights and liabilities of consumers as well as the responsibilities of all participants in electronic funds transfer activities. The act was implemented in Federal Reserve Board (FRB) Regulation E. Rulemaking authority under EFTA generally transferred from the FRB to the CFPB in July 2011 pursuant to the Dodd-Frank Act.[18]

Regulation E contains two subparts—A and B:

- *Subpart A* contains regulations that apply to electronic fund transfers (EFTs), prepaid accounts, gift cards, and gift certificates. Subpart A's regulations applicable to EFTs include disclosures, error resolution, and rules related to unauthorized EFTs. The regulations applicable to gift cards and certificates include disclosures and limitations on fees and expiration dates.
- *Subpart B* to Regulation E contains rules regarding remittance transfers (the Remittance Rule). These rules provide for disclosure, error resolution, and cancellation rights.

Equal Credit Opportunity Act

The Equal Credit Opportunity Act (ECOA), which is implemented by Regulation B of the Federal Reserve, applies to all creditors. When originally enacted in 1974, ECOA gave the Federal Reserve Board responsibility for prescribing the implementing regulation. The Dodd-Frank Act of 2010 transferred this authority to the CFPB.

In January 2013, the CFPB amended Regulation B to reflect the Dodd-Frank Act amendments requiring creditors to provide applicants with free copies of all appraisals and other written valuations developed in connection with all credit applications to be secured by a first lien on a dwelling. This amendment to Regulation B also requires creditors to notify applicants in writing that copies of all appraisals will be provided to them promptly.

The statute provides that its purpose is to require financial institutions and other firms engaged in the extension of credit to "make credit equally available to all creditworthy customers without regard to sex or

---

[18] Consumer Financial Protection Bureau, "Electronic Fund Transfers (Regulation E); Amendments," https://www.consumerfinance.gov/policy-compliance/rulemaking/final-rules/electronic-fund-transfers-regulation-e

marital status." Moreover, the statute makes it unlawful for "any creditor to discriminate against any applicant with respect to any aspect of a credit transaction:

- On the basis of race, color, religion, national origin, sex or marital status, or age (provided the applicant has the capacity to contract), or
- Because all or part of the applicant's income derives from any public assistance program, or
- Because the applicant has in good faith exercised any right under the Consumer Credit Protection Act"[19]

The courts have recognized three methods of proof of lending discrimination under ECOA:[20]

- *Overt Evidence of Discrimination* occurs when a creditor openly discriminates on a prohibited basis or makes statements indicating a discriminatory preference. There is overt evidence of discrimination even when a creditor does not act on the stated discriminatory preference.
- *Disparate Treatment* occurs when a creditor treats an applicant differently based on one of the prohibited bases. It does not require any showing that the treatment was motivated by prejudice or a conscious intent to discriminate against a person beyond the difference in treatment itself.
- *Disparate Impact* occurs when a creditor employs a neutral policy or practice equally to all credit applicants, but the policy or practice disproportionately excludes or burdens certain persons on a prohibited basis. Even if a policy or practice that has a disparate impact on a prohibited basis can be justified by business necessity, it still may be found to be in violation if an alternative policy or practice could serve the same purpose with less discriminatory effect. Finally, evidence of discriminatory intent is not necessary to establish that a lender's adoption or implementation of a policy or practice that has a disparate impact is in violation of ECOA.

---

[19] National Credit Union Administration, "Equal Credit Opportunity Act (Regulation B)," https://www.ncua.gov/regulation-supervision/manuals-guides/federal-consumer-financial-protection-guide/compliance-management/lending-regulations/equal-credit-opportunity-act-regulation-b

[20] Consumer Financial Protection Bureau, "Equal Credit Opportunity Act: Baseline Review Models," https://files.consumerfinance.gov/f/documents/cfpb_supervision-and-examination-manual_ecoa-baseline-exam-procedures_2019-04.pdf

In keeping with the broad reach of the statute's prohibition, the regulation covers creditor activities before, during, and after the extension of credit.[21]

Table 9.4 reviews sample CDEs for ECOA compliance.

Table 9.4: CDEs for ECOA compliance

Critical data element	Definition
1. Color	Protected category.
2. Religion	Protected category.
3. National Origin	Protected category.
4. Sex	Protected category.
5. Alimony, Child Support, or Separate Maintenance Income	A creditor may ask if an applicant is receiving alimony, child support, or separate maintenance payments. However, the creditor must first disclose to the applicant that such income need not be revealed unless the applicant wishes to rely on that income in the determination of creditworthiness. An appropriate notice to that effect must be given whenever the creditor makes a general request concerning income and the source of that income. Therefore, a creditor either must ask questions designed to solicit only information about specific income (for example, "salary," "wages," "employment," or other specified categories of income) or must state that disclosure of alimony, child support, or separate maintenance payments is not required.
6. Child-bearing or Child-rearing information, assumptions, or statistics	Generally, a creditor may not use child-bearing or child-rearing information, assumptions, or statistics to determine whether an applicant's income may be interrupted or decreased..
7. Age	Generally, a creditor may not consider any of the prohibited bases, including age (providing the applicant is old enough, under state law, to enter into a binding contract).

Figure 9.4 shows sample CDEs for ECOA in YourDataConnect.

[21] Bureau of Consumer Financial Protection, "Equal Credit Opportunity Act (ECOA)," https://files.consumerfinance.gov/f/documents/201510_cfpb_ecoa-narrative-and-procedures.pdf

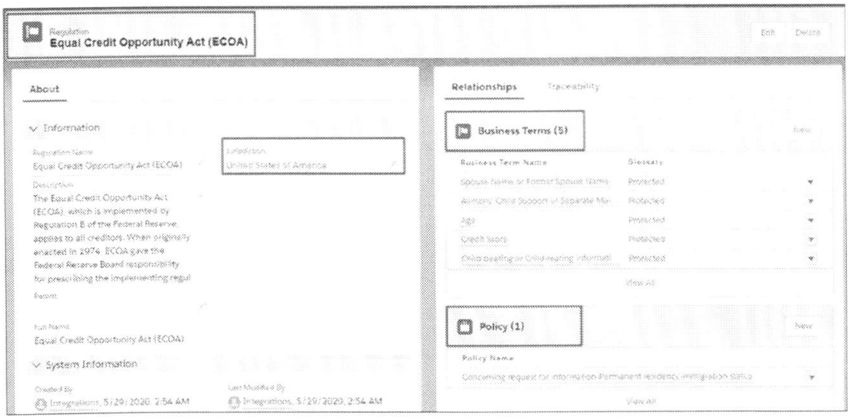

Figure 9.4: ECOA CDEs in YourDataConnect

Fair Credit Reporting Act

The Fair Credit Reporting Act (FCRA) became effective on April 25, 1971. The FCRA is a part of a group of acts contained in the Federal Consumer Credit Protection Act (CCPA) such as the Truth in Lending Act and the Fair Debt Collection Practices Act. Congress substantially amended the FCRA upon the passage of the Fair and Accurate Credit Transactions Act of 2003 (FACT Act). The FACT Act created many new responsibilities for consumer reporting agencies and users of consumer reports. It contained many new consumer disclosure requirements as well as provisions to address identity theft. In addition, it provided free annual consumer report rights for consumers and improved access to consumer report information to help increase the accuracy of data in the consumer reporting system. In 2010, Congress passed the Dodd-Frank Wall Street Reform and Consumer Protection Act, which granted primary rule-making authority under FCRA to the CFPB. The Dodd-Frank Act also amended two provisions of the FCRA to require the disclosure of a credit score and related information when a credit score is used in taking an adverse action or in risk-based pricing.

FCRA contains responsibilities both for entities that are consumer reporting agencies and for persons that operate in any of the following capacities:

- Procurers and users of information (for example, as credit grantors, purchasers of dealer paper, or when opening deposit accounts)
- Furnishers and transmitters of information (by reporting information to consumer reporting agencies, other third parties, or to affiliates)
- Marketers of credit or insurance products
- Employers[22]

FCRA contains many substantive compliance requirements for consumer reporting agencies designed to help ensure the accuracy and integrity of the consumer reporting system. FCRA defines a consumer reporting agency as a person that generally furnishes consumer reports to third parties. By their very nature, third parties such as banks, credit unions, and other financial institutions have a significant amount of consumer information that could constitute a consumer report, and thus communication of this information could cause the institution to become a consumer reporting agency.

FCRA contains several exceptions that enable parties, such as a financial institution, to communicate this type of information, within strict guidelines, without becoming a consumer reporting agency. Rather than containing strict information-sharing prohibitions, the FCRA creates a business disincentive such that if an entity shares consumer report information outside the exceptions, then the institution is a consumer reporting agency and will be subject to the significant, substantive requirements of the FCRA applicable to those entities. Typically, an entity such as a financial institution will structure its information-sharing practices within the exceptions to avoid becoming a consumer reporting agency.[23]

As Figure 9.5 shows, YourDataConnect supports a number of out-of-the-box and custom workflows, including for data sharing. These data sharing workflows can be configured so that data owners can obtain the necessary approvals before sharing data in a manner that does not trigger the organization to be classified as a consumer reporting agency.

---

[22] Consumer Financial Protection Bureau, "Fair Credit Reporting Act," https://files.consumerfinance.gov/f/documents/102012_cfpb_fair-credit-reporting-act-fcra_procedures.pdf

[23] Federal Deposit Insurance Corporation, "Fair Credit Reporting Act," *Consumer Compliance Examination Manual*, https://www.fdic.gov/regulations/compliance/manual/8/viii-6.1.pdf

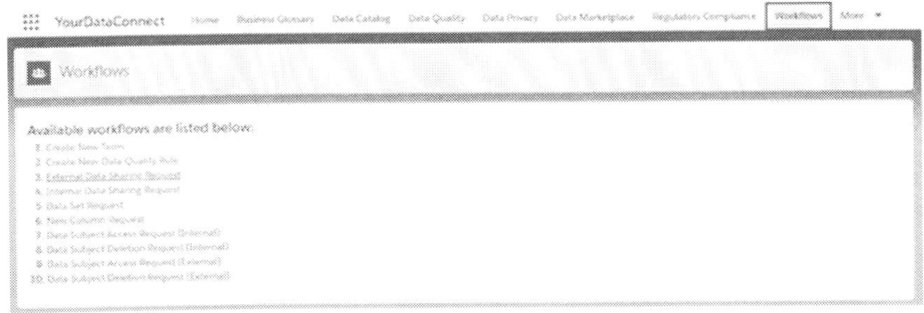

Figure 9.5: YourDataConnect supports data sharing workflows

Fair Debt Collection Practices Act

The Fair Debt Collection Practices Act (FDCPA) of 1978, was designed to eliminate abusive, deceptive, and unfair debt collection practices. In addition, the federal law protects reputable debt collectors from unfair competition and encourages consistent state action to protect consumers from abuses in debt collection. The Dodd-Frank Act moved enforcement and rulemaking authority under the FDCPA from the Federal Trade Commission to the CFPB.

The FDCPA applies only to the collection of debt incurred by a consumer primarily for personal, family, or household purposes. It does not apply to the collection of corporate debt or to debt owed for business or agricultural purposes.[24]

Gramm-Leach-Bliley Act

Title V, Subtitle A of the Gramm-Leach-Bliley Act (GLBA) governs the treatment of nonpublic personal information about consumers by financial institutions. Section 502 of the Subtitle, subject to certain exceptions, prohibits a financial institution from disclosing nonpublic personal information about a consumer to non-affiliated third parties, unless (i) the institution satisfies various notice and opt-out requirements and (ii) the consumer has not elected to opt out of the disclosure.

Section 503 requires the institution to provide notice of its privacy policies and practices to its customers. Section 504 authorizes the issuance of regulations to implement these provisions. Title X of the Dodd-Frank

[24] Consumer Financial Protection Bureau, "Fair Debt Collection Practices Act," https://files.consumerfinance.gov/f/documents/102012_cfpb_fair-debt-collections-practices-act-fdcpa_procedures.pdf

Act granted rulemaking authority for most provisions of Subtitle A of Title V of GLBA to the CFPB with respect to financial institutions and other entities subject to the CFPB's jurisdiction, except securities- and futures-related companies and certain motor vehicle dealers. The Dodd-Frank Act also granted authority to the CFPB to examine and enforce compliance with these statutory provisions and their implementing regulations with respect to entities under CFPB jurisdiction.

The regulation establishes rules governing duties of a financial institution to provide particular notices and limitations on its disclosure of nonpublic personal information, as summarized below:

- A financial institution must provide notice of its privacy policies and practices and allow the consumer to opt out of the disclosure of the consumer's nonpublic personal information to a non-affiliated third party if the disclosure is outside of certain exceptions. If the financial institution provides the consumer's nonpublic personal information to a non-affiliated third party under the exception in Section 13, it must provide notice of its privacy policies and practices to the consumer. Under the exception in Section 13, the financial institution must also enter into a contractual agreement with the third party that prohibits the third party from disclosing or using the information other than to perform services for the institution or functions on the institution's behalf, including use under an exception in Sections 14 or 15 in the ordinary course of business to carry out those services or functions. If the financial institution complies with these requirements, it is not required to provide an opt-out notice.
- Regardless of whether a financial institution shares nonpublic personal information, the institution must provide notice of its privacy policies and practices to its customers.
- A financial institution generally may not disclose consumer account numbers to any non-affiliated third party for marketing purposes.
- A financial institution must follow redisclosure and reuse limitations on any nonpublic personal information it receives from a non-affiliated financial institution.

In general, the privacy notice must describe a financial institution's policies and practices with respect to collecting and disclosing nonpublic personal information about a consumer to both affiliated and non-affiliated third parties. Also, the notice must provide a consumer a reasonable opportunity to direct the institution generally not to share nonpublic personal information about the consumer (that is, to "opt out") with non-affiliated third parties other than as permitted by exceptions under the regulation (for example, sharing for everyday business purposes, such as processing transactions and maintaining customers' accounts, and in response to properly executed governmental requests). The privacy notice must also provide, where applicable under the Fair Credit Reporting Act, a notice and an opportunity for a consumer to opt out of certain information sharing among affiliates.[25]

Table 9.5 reviews sample CDEs for GLBA.

Table 9.5: CDEs for GLBA compliance

Critical data element	Definition
1. Affiliate	An affiliate of a financial institution is any company that controls, is controlled by, or is under common control with the financial institution.
2. Non-Public Information	Nonpublic personal information generally is any information that is not publicly available and that: • A consumer provides to a financial institution to obtain a financial product or service from the institution; • Results from a transaction between the consumer and the institution involving a financial product or service; or • A financial institution otherwise obtains about a consumer in connection with providing a financial product or service. Information is publicly available if an institution has a reasonable basis to believe that the information is lawfully made available to the general public from government records, widely distributed media, or legally required disclosures to the general public. Examples include information in a telephone book or a publicly recorded document, such as a mortgage or security interest filing.
3. Opt-Out	Consumers must be given the right to "opt out" of, or prevent, a financial institution from disclosing nonpublic personal information about them to a non-affiliated third party unless an exception to that right applies. As part of the opt-out right, consumers must be given a reasonable opportunity and a reasonable means to opt out. What constitutes a reasonable opportunity to opt out depends on the circumstances surrounding the consumer's transaction, but a consumer must be provided a reasonable amount of time to exercise the opt-out right. For example, it would be reasonable if the financial institution allows 30 days from the date of mailing a notice or 30 days after customer acknowledgment of an electronic notice for an opt-out direction to be returned. What constitutes a reasonable means to opt out may include check-off boxes, a reply form, or a toll-free telephone number. It is not reasonable to require a consumer to write his or her own letter as the only means to opt out.

[25] "Gramm-Leach-Bliley Act (GLBA): Consumer Financial Protection Bureau, "Privacy of Consumer Financial Information," https://files.consumerfinance.gov/f/documents/102016_cfpb_GLBAExamManualUpdate.pdf

Figure 9.6 shows sample GLBA CDEs in YourDataConnect.

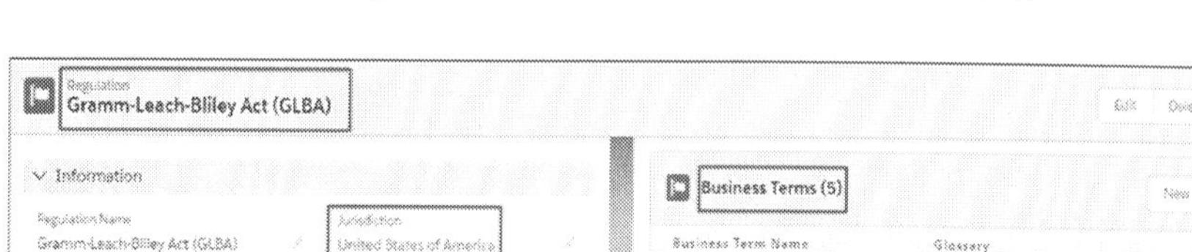

Figure 9.6: GLBA-related business terms in YourDataConnect

Home Mortgage Disclosure Act

The Home Mortgage Disclosure Act (HMDA) was enacted by Congress in 1975 and was implemented by the Federal Reserve Board's Regulation C. On July 21, 2011, the rule-writing authority of Regulation C was transferred to the CFPB. HMDA provides public loan data that can be used to assist:

- In determining whether financial institutions are serving the housing needs of their communities
- Public officials in distributing public-sector investments so as to attract private investment to areas where it is needed
- In identifying possible discriminatory lending patterns

This regulation applies to certain financial institutions, including banks, savings associations, credit unions, and other mortgage lending institutions.[26]

Table 9.6 shows sample CDEs for HMDA compliance.

[26] Federal Financial Institutions Examination Council, "Filing instructions guide for HMDA data collected in 2020," https://s3.amazonaws.com/cfpb-hmda-public/prod/help/2020-hmda-fig.pdf

Table 9.6: CDEs for HMDA compliance

Critical data element	Guidance from HMDA filing instructions[27]
1. Universal Loan Identifier (ULI) or Non-Universal Loan Identifier (NULI)	This number is a combination of the following: • Begins with the financial institution's Legal Entity Identifier (LEI) • Followed by up to 23 additional characters to identify the covered loan or application, which: o May be letters, numerals, or a combination of letters and numerals, o Must be unique within the financial institution, and o Must not include any information that could be used to directly identify the applicant or borrower. • Ends with a two-character check digit that is calculated using the ISO/IEC 7064, MOD 97-10 as it appears on the International Standard ISO/IEC 7064:2003, which is published by the International Organization for Standardization (ISO) • Example: 10BX 939C5543T QA1144M999143X38
2. Loan Type	Indicates the type of covered loan or application by entering the applicable code from the following: • Code 1—Conventional (not insured or guaranteed by the Federal Housing Administration (FHA), Veterans Affairs (VA), United States Department of Agriculture Rural Housing Service (USDA RHS), or Farm Service Agency (FSA)) • Code 2—Federal Housing Administration (FHA) insured • Code 3—Veterans Affairs guaranteed (VA) • Code 4—USDA Rural Housing Service (RHS) or Farm Service Agency (FSA) guaranteed
3. Loan Purpose	Indicates the purpose of the covered loan or application by entering the applicable code from the following: • Code 1—Home purchase • Code 2—Home improvement • Code 31—Refinancing • Code 32—Cash-out refinancing • Code 4—Other purpose • Code 5—Not applicable
4. Preapproval	Indicates whether the covered loan or application involved a request for a preapproval of a home purchase loan under a preapproval program by entering the applicable code from the following: • Code 1—Pre-approval requested • Code 2—Pre-approval not requested
5. Construction Method	Indicates the construction method for the dwelling by entering the applicable code from the following: • Code 1—Site-built • Code 2—Manufactured home

[27] Ibid.

Figure 9.7 shows sample HMDA CDEs in YourDataConnect.

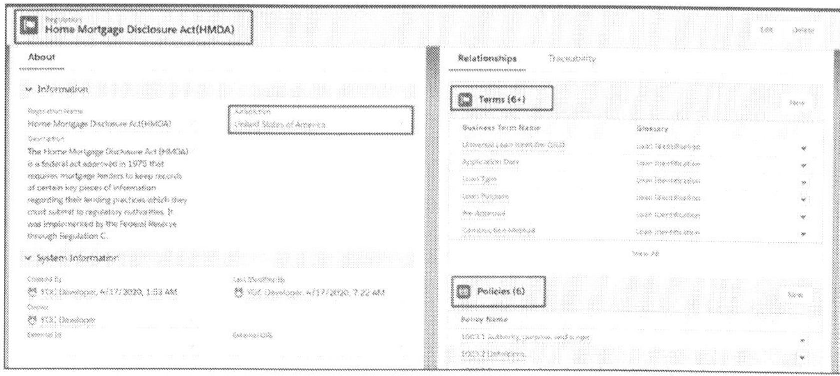

Figure 9.7: Sample HMDA CDEs in YourDataConnect

Table 9.7 describes sample data quality rules for HMDA.[28]

Table 9.7: Data quality rules for HMDA compliance	
Critical data element	**Data quality rule**
1. ULI	If Action Taken equals “Loan Originated”, then a duplicate ULI cannot be reported.
2. Application Date	Application Date must be either a valid date using YYYYMMDD format or NA and cannot be left blank.
3. Action Taken, Application Date	If Action Taken equals “Purchased loan”, then Application Date must be NA, and the reverse must be true.
4. Loan Purpose, Preapproval	If Preapproval equals “Pre Approval Requested”, then Loan Purpose must equal “Home Purchase”.
5. Occupancy Type	Occupancy Type must equal principal residence, second residence, or investment property and cannot be left blank.

Figure 9.8 shows the HMDA data quality rules associated with ULI in YourDataConnect.

[28] Ibid.

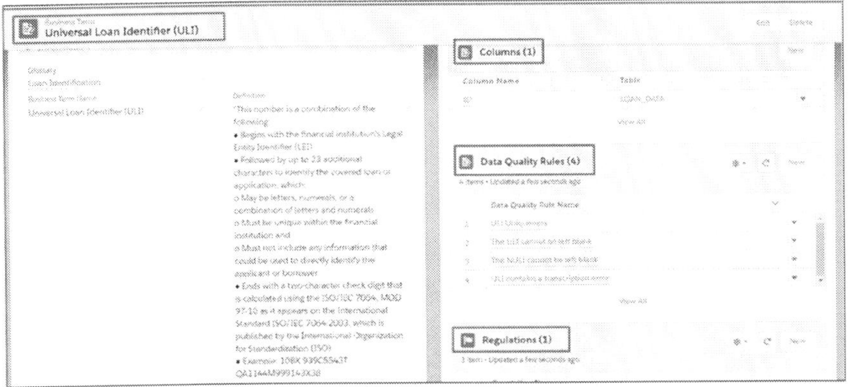

Figure 9.8: HMDA data quality rules associated with ULI in YourDataConnect

Homeowners Protection Act

The Homeowners Protection Act of 1998 (HPA), or PMI Cancellation Act, became effective on July 29, 1999. The HPA addresses homeowners' difficulties in canceling private mortgage insurance (PMI) coverage. It establishes provisions for canceling and terminating PMI, sets disclosure and notification requirements, and requires the return of unearned premiums.

The Dodd-Frank Act granted authority to the CFPB to supervise and enforce compliance with the HPA with respect to entities within its jurisdiction. PMI is insurance that protects lenders from the risk of default and foreclosure. PMI enables prospective buyers who cannot, or choose not to, provide significant down payments to obtain mortgage financing at affordable rates. It is used extensively to facilitate "high-ratio" loans (generally, loans in which the loan to value, or LTV, ratio exceeds 80 percent). With PMI, the lender can recover costs associated with the resale of foreclosed property as well as accrued interest payments or fixed costs, such as taxes or insurance policies, paid prior to resale.

Excessive PMI coverage provides little extra protection for a lender and does not benefit the borrower. In some instances, homeowners have experienced problems in canceling PMI. At other times, lenders may have agreed to terminate coverage when the borrower's equity reached 20 percent, but the policies and procedures used for canceling or terminating PMI coverage varied widely among lenders. Before the HPA, homeowners had limited recourse when lenders refused to cancel their PMI coverage. Even homeowners in the few states with laws pertaining to PMI cancellation or termination noted difficulties in canceling or terminating their PMI policies. The act now protects homeowners by prohibiting life-of-loan PMI coverage for borrower-paid PMI products and by establishing uniform procedures for the cancellation and termination of PMI policies.[29]

Real Estate Settlement Procedures Act

The Real Estate Settlement Procedures Act (RESPA) was a law passed by the U.S. Congress in 1974. Its main objective was to protect homeowners by helping them become better educated while shopping for real estate services and eliminating kickbacks and referral fees that add unnecessary costs to settlement services. RESPA requires lenders and others involved in mortgage lending to give borrowers pertinent and timely disclosures about the nature and costs of a real estate settlement process. RESPA was also designed to prohibit potentially abusive practices such as kickbacks and referral fees and the practice of dual tracking, and it imposes limitations on the use of escrow accounts.

RESPA was originally administered by the Department of Housing and Urban Development (HUD). In 2011, the CFPB assumed enforcement and rule-making authority over RESPA. On December 31, 2013, the CFPB published final rules implementing provisions of the Dodd-Frank Act that direct the CFPB to publish a single, integrated disclosure for mortgage transactions, which included mortgage disclosure requirements under the Truth in Lending Act and Sections 4 and 5 of RESPA. As a result, Regulation Z now houses the integrated forms, timing, and related disclosure requirements for most closed-end consumer mortgage loans.[30]

---

[29] Consumer Financial Protection Bureau, "Homeowners Protection Act (PMI Cancellation Act)," https://files.consumerfinance.gov/f/documents/102012_cfpb_homeowners-protection-act-hpa-pmi-cancellation-act_procedures.pdf

[30] Wikipedia, "Real Estate Settlement Procedures Act," https://en.wikipedia.org/wiki/Real_Estate_Settlement_Procedures_Act

Secure and Fair Enforcement for Mortgage Licensing Act

The Secure and Fair Enforcement for Mortgage Licensing Act of 2008 (SAFE Act) was enacted on July 30, 2008. It mandates a nationwide licensing and registration system for residential mortgage loan originators (MLOs). The SAFE Act prohibits individuals from engaging in the business of a residential mortgage loan originator without first obtaining and maintaining annually:

- For individuals who are employees of a covered financial institution, registration as a registered mortgage loan originator and a unique identifier (federal registration), or
- For all other individuals, a state license and registration as a state-licensed mortgage loan originator, and a unique identifier (state licensing/registration).

The SAFE Act requires federal registration and state licensing and registration to be accomplished through the Nationwide Mortgage Licensing System (NMLS). The Dodd-Frank Act transferred rule-making and enforcement authority for SAFE and similar regulations from the Office of the Comptroller of the Currency (OCC), Federal Reserve Board, Federal Deposit Insurance Corporation, Office of Thrift Supervision (OTS), National Credit Union Administration (NCUA), Farm Credit Administration (FCA), and the U.S. Department of Housing and Urban Development to the CFPB.[31]

Table 9.8 shows a sample CDE for the SAFE Act.

Table 9.8: CDE for SAFE Act compliance

CDE	Definition
1. NMLS Number	Unique identifier for mortgage originators within the Nationwide Mortgage Licensing System to track individuals who might move between companies and states

[31] Consumer Financial Protection Bureau, "Secure and Fair Enforcement for Mortgage Licensing Act," https://files.consumerfinance.gov/f/documents/102012_cfpb_secure-fair-enforcement-for-mortgage-licensing-safe-act_procedures.pdf

Truth in Lending Act

The Truth in Lending Act (TILA) of 1968 is a U.S. federal law designed to promote the informed use of consumer credit by requiring disclosures about its terms and cost to standardize the manner in which costs associated with borrowing are calculated and disclosed.

TILA also gives consumers the right to cancel certain credit transactions that involve a lien on a consumer's principal dwelling, regulates certain credit card practices, and provides a means for fair and timely resolution of credit billing disputes. With the exception of certain high-cost mortgage loans, TILA does not regulate the charges that may be imposed for consumer credit. Rather, it requires uniform or standardized disclosure of costs and charges so that consumers can shop. It also imposes limitations on home equity plans and certain "higher-priced mortgage loans" (HPMLs). The regulation prohibits certain acts or practices in connection with credit secured by a consumer's principal dwelling.

Enacted on May 29, 1968, TILA was originally Title I of the Consumer Credit Protection Act. The regulations implementing the statute are known as Regulation Z. Most of the specific requirements imposed by TILA are found in Regulation Z, so a reference to the requirements of TILA usually refers to the requirements contained in Regulation Z as well as the statute itself.

From TILA's inception, the authority to implement the statute by issuing regulations was given to the Federal Reserve Board. However, effective July 21, 2011, TILA's general-rule making authority was transferred to the CFPB. The TILA introduced the Annual Percentage Rate (APR) calculation mandated for all consumer lenders. Certain misleading interest rate calculations used previously, mainly on auto loans, were barred.[32]

Table 9.9 reviews sample CDEs for TILA.[33]

---

[32] Wikipedia, "Truth in Lending Act," https://en.wikipedia.org/wiki/Truth_in_Lending_Act

[33] Consumer Financial Protection Bureau, "Truth in Lending Act," https://files.consumerfinance.gov/f/documents/cfpb_supervision-and-examination-manual_tila-exam-procedures_2019-03.pdf

Table 9.9: CDE for TILA compliance	
Critical data element	**Definition/supervisory guidance**
1. Finance Charge (Closed-End Credit)	The amount financed is the net amount of credit extended for the consumer's use. It should not be assumed that the amount financed under the regulation is equivalent to the note amount, proceeds, or principal amount of the loan. The amount financed normally equals the total of payments less the finance charge. Example: A consumer signs a note secured by real property in the amount of $5,435. The note amount includes $5,000 in proceeds disbursed to the consumer, $400 in precomputed interest, $25 paid to a credit reporting agency for a credit report, and a $10 service charge. In addition, the consumer pays a $50 loan fee separately in cash at consummation. The consumer has no other debt with the financial institution. The amount financed is $4,975. The amount financed may be calculated by first subtracting all finance charges included in the note amount ($5,435 – $400 – $10 = $5,025). The $25 credit report fee is not a finance charge because the loan is secured by real property. The $5,025 is further reduced by the amount of prepaid finance charges paid separately, for an amount financed of $5,025 – $50 = $4,975.
2. Annual Percentage Rate (Closed-End Credit)	The annual percentage rate is a measure of the cost of credit, expressed as a yearly rate, that relates the amount and timing of value received by the consumer to the amount and timing of payments made. The annual percentage rate shall be determined in accordance with either the actuarial method or the United States Rule method.
3. Required Deposit (Closed-End Credit)	A required deposit, with certain exceptions, is one that the financial institution requires the consumer to maintain as a condition of the specific credit transaction. It can include a compensating balance or a deposit balance that secures the loan. The effect of a required deposit is not reflected in the APR. Also, a required deposit is not a finance charge since it is eventually released to the consumer. A deposit that earns at least 5 percent per year need not be considered a required deposit.
4. Sale Price	(i) For transactions that involve a seller, the contract sale price of the property, labeled "Sale Price". (ii) For transactions that do not involve a seller, the estimated value of the property, labeled "Property Value".
5. Prepayment Penalty	A charge imposed for paying all or part of a transaction's principal before the date on which the principal is due, other than a waived, bona fide third-party charge that the creditor imposes if the consumer prepays all of the transaction's principal sooner than 36 months after consummation.
6. Balloon Payment	A payment that is more than two times a regular periodic payment. "Balloon payment" includes the payment or payments under a transaction that requires only one or two payments during the loan term.

Figure 9.9 shows sample TILA CDEs in YourDataConnect.

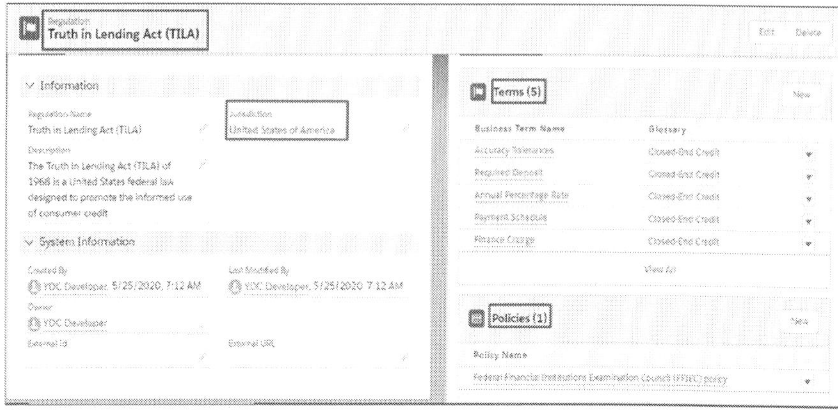

Figure 9.9: Sample TILA CDEs in YourDataConnect

Truth in Savings Act

Regulation DD, which implements the Truth in Savings Act (TISA), took effect in June 1993. The Dodd-Frank Act granted enforcement and rulemaking authority under TISA to the CFPB. The purpose of Regulation DD is to enable consumers to make informed decisions about their accounts at depository institutions through the use of uniform disclosures. The disclosures aid comparison shopping by informing consumers about the fees, annual percentage yield, interest rate, and other terms for deposit accounts. A consumer is entitled to receive disclosures under all of the following circumstances:

- When an account is opened
- Upon request
- When the terms of the account are changed
- When a periodic statement is sent
- For most time accounts, before the account matures

The regulation also includes requirements on the payment of interest, the methods of calculating the balance on which interest is paid, the calculation of the annual-percentage yield, and advertising.[34]

[34] Consumer Financial Protection Bureau, "Truth in Savings Act," https://files.consumerfinance.gov/f/documents/102012_cfpb_truth-savings-act-tisa_procedures.pdf

Table 9.10 reviews sample CDEs for TISA compliance.

Table 9.10: CDEs for TISA compliance

Critical data element	Definition
1. Annual Percentage Yield (APY)	Percentage rate reflecting the total amount of interest paid on an account, based on the interest rate and the frequency of compounding for a 365-day period, or a 366-day period during leap years, and calculated according to the rules in Appendix A of Regulation DD.
2. Bonus	Premium, gift, award, or other consideration worth more than $10 (whether in the form of cash, credit, merchandise, or any equivalent) given or offered to a consumer during a year in exchange for opening, maintaining, renewing, or increasing an account balance. (The term does not include interest, other consideration worth $10 or less given during a year, the waiver or reduction of a fee, or the absorption of expenses.)
3. Grace Period	Period following the maturity of an automatically renewing time account during which the consumer may withdraw funds without being assessed a penalty.
4. Minimum Balance	Minimum balance required to be maintained in the account to assess fees or earn interest.
5. Fee	An institution must disclose the amount of any fee that may be imposed in connection with the account (or an explanation of how the fee will be determined) and the conditions under which the fee may be imposed. Examples of fees that must be disclosed are: • Maintenance fees, such as monthly service fees • Fees to open or close an account • Fees related to deposits or withdrawals, such as fees for use of the institution's ATMs • Fees for special services, such as stop-payment fees
6. Dormant Account	Based on applicable state law.

Figure 9.10 shows the TISA CDEs in YourDataConnect.

Unfair, Deceptive, or Abusive Acts or Practices

Unfair, deceptive, or abusive acts or practices (UDAAPs) can cause significant financial injury to consumers, erode consumer confidence, and undermine the financial marketplace. Under the Dodd-Frank Act, it is unlawful for any provider of consumer financial products or services or a service provider to engage in any unfair, deceptive, or abusive act or practice. The act also gives the CFPB rule-making authority and, with respect to entities within its jurisdiction, enforcement authority to prevent unfair,

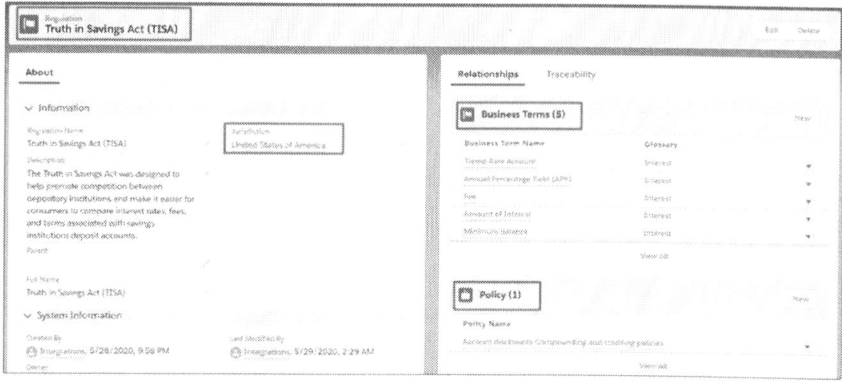

Figure 9.10: TISA CDEs in YourDataConnect

deceptive, or abusive acts or practices in connection with any transaction with a consumer for a consumer financial product or service, or the offering of a consumer financial product or service. In addition, CFPB has supervisory authority for detecting and assessing risks to consumers and to markets for consumer financial products and services.[35]

Summary

Consumer protection law, or consumer law, is an area of law that regulates private law relationships between individual consumers and the businesses that sell them goods and services. Consumer protection covers a wide range of topics, including but not necessarily limited to product liability, privacy rights, unfair business practices, fraud, misrepresentation, and other interactions between consumers and businesses. The United States, the European Union, and other jurisdictions have a number of consumer protection laws, some of which are data-intensive from a compliance perspective.

[35] Consumer Financial Protection Bureau, "Unfair, Deceptive, or Abusive Acts or Practices," https://files.consumerfinance.gov/f/documents/102012_cfpb_unfair-deceptive-abusive-acts-practices-udaaps_procedures.pdf

10

Financial Services Regulations

Financial services firms have to comply with several regulations. These regulations require strong data management practices and include the following:

- Bank Secrecy Act/Anti-Money Laundering (BSA/AML)
- Comprehensive Capital Analysis and Review (CCAR)
- Current Expected Credit Loss (CECL)
- Office of Foreign Assets Control (OFAC)
- Financial Crimes Enforcement Network (FinCEN)

Bank Secrecy Act/Anti-Money Laundering

The U.S. Treasury Department's Treasury Order 180-01 empowers the Financial Crimes Enforcement Network (FinCEN) bureau with the implementation, administration, and enforcement of the articles contained in the BSA/AML law. The BSA/AML law requires U.S. financial organizations to assist government agencies in the detection and prevention of money laundering activities by helping to identify the source, volume, and movement of currency and other monetary instruments transported or transmitted into or out of the United States or deposited into U.S. financial institutions. The act requires financial institutions to keep records of cash purchases of negotiable instruments, report cash transactions exceeding $10,000, and report suspicious activity that may signify money laundering, tax evasion, and other criminal activities.

The Money Laundering Control Act of 1986 augmented the BSA/AML law by adding provisions found in Sections 8(s) and 21 of the Federal Deposit Insurance Act and Section 206(q) of the Federal Credit Union Act. These provisions impose criminal liability on a person or financial institution that knowingly assists in the laundering of money, or that structures transactions to avoid reporting them. The act directs banks to establish and maintain procedures designed to ensure and monitor compliance with the reporting and recordkeeping requirements of the AML law.

The Annunzio-Wylie Anti-Money Laundering Act of 1992 strengthened the AML law by imposing more stringent sanctions for BSA/AML law violations and enhancing the role of the U.S. Treasury. Treasury's role in combating money laundering was further enhanced by the Money Laundering Suppression Act of 1994.

In 1996, the standardized Suspicious Activity Report (SAR) was developed. All banking organizations are required to submit a SAR when a known or suspected criminal violation of federal law, a suspicious transaction related to money laundering, or a violation of the BSA/AML law is detected.

Title III of the USA PATRIOT Act is the International Money Laundering Abatement and Anti-Terrorist Financing Act of 2001. This act criminalizes the financing of terrorism and augments the BSA/AML law by:

- Strengthening customer identification procedures
- Prohibiting financial institutions from engaging in business with foreign shell banks
- Requiring financial institutions to have due diligence or enhanced due diligence procedures for foreign correspondent and private banking accounts
- Improving information sharing between financial institutions and the U.S. government
- Expanding the AML program requirements to include all financial institutions
- Increasing the civil and criminal penalties for money laundering
- Providing the Secretary of the Treasury with the authority to impose special measures on jurisdictions, institutions, or transactions that are of concern

AML regulations require all financial institutions to develop a BSA/AML compliance program commensurate with their BSA/AML risk profile. This profile is generally determined by the assessing the institution's exposure to specific risk categories:

- Products and services such as electronic funds payment services, domestic and international private banking, foreign correspondent accounts, and trust and asset management services

- Customers and entities such as foreign financial institutions, non-bank financial institutions, shell companies, non-governmental organizations, and professional service providers
- Geographic locations such as countries subject to OFAC sanctions and jurisdictions subject to special measures imposed by the Secretary of the Treasury

Table 10.1 reviews sample CDEs for BSA/AML.

Table 10.1: CDEs for BSA/AML compliance

Data category	Critical data elements
1. Customer Identification Program	• First Name • Middle Name • Last Name • Date of Birth • Occupation • National Origin • Social Security Number • Passport Number • Street Address • City • State • Zip or Postal Code • Country
2. Financial Institution	• Organization Name • Doing Business As (DBA) Name • Taxpayer Identification Number (TIN) • Legal Entity Identifier (LEI) • Entity Type • Parent Name • Ultimate Parent Name • Subsidiary Name • North American Industry Classification System (NAICS) code
3. Transactions	• Transaction Type (e.g., Wire Transfer, ATM Withdrawal, Direct Deposit) • Transaction Amount • Transaction Date • Sender Name • Recipient Name • Financial Institution Name (Sender, Recipient, Correspondent)

Figure 10.1 shows AML CDEs in YourDataConnect™.

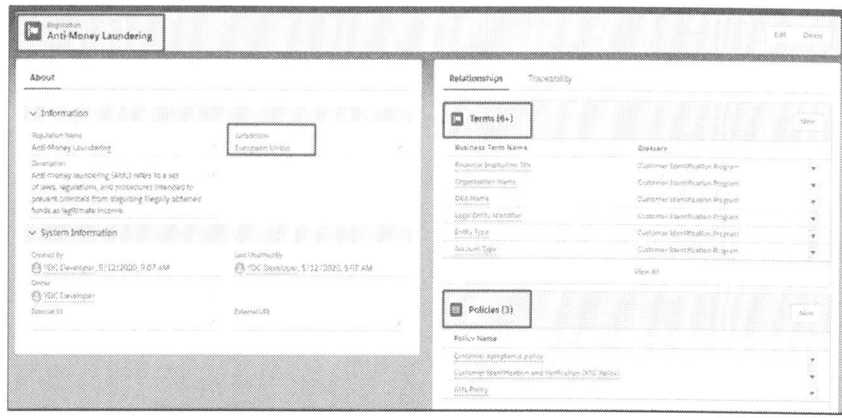

Figure 10.1: AML CDEs in YourDataConnect™

Table 10.2 describes sample data quality rules for BSA/AML.

Table 10.2: Data quality rules for BSA/AML compliance	
Critical data element	**Data quality rule**
1. Social Security Number	Social Security Number must be unique to an individual or organization
2. Taxpayer Identification Number	Taxpayer Identification Number must be unique to an organization
3. Date of Birth	Date of Birth cannot be null and cannot be more than 110 years ago

Comprehensive Capital Analysis and Review

The U.S. Federal Reserve, through its supervision and regulation of banking organizations, is tasked with promoting a safe, sound, and efficient banking and financial system. Annual assessment of the capital adequacy and capital planning practices of the largest and most complex banking organizations is a key component of that oversight. Such assessment allows the Federal Reserve to determine whether bank holding companies (BHCs) and U.S. intermediate holding companies of foreign banking organizations (IHCs) have sufficient capital to continue operating and lending to households and businesses, even during times of economic and financial market stress.

This annual assessment consists of two primary components:

- The Dodd-Frank Act Stress Test (DFAST) is a forward-looking quantitative evaluation of bank capital that demonstrates how a hypothetical set of stressful economic conditions developed by the Federal Reserve would affect the capital ratios of large firms.
- The Comprehensive Capital Analysis and Review (CCAR) exercise includes a quantitative assessment for all subject firms and a qualitative assessment of the capital planning practices of the largest and most complex firms' capital planning practices. The CCAR quantitative assessment uses the same results as DFAST and incorporates firms' planned capital actions, such as dividend payments and common stock repurchases. In the qualitative assessment, the Federal Reserve evaluates how the largest and most complex firms identify, measure, and determine capital needs for their material risks. At the conclusion of the process, the Federal Reserve can object to all subject firms' capital plans on quantitative grounds and certain firms' capital plans on qualitative grounds.[36]

Figure 10.2 shows sample CDEs for CCAR.

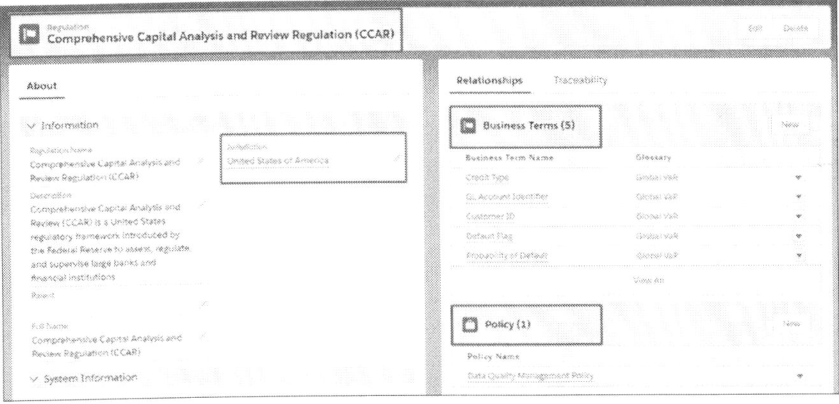

Figure 10.2: Sample CDEs for CCAR

[36] Board of Governors of the Federal Reserve System, *Comprehensive Capital Analysis and Review 2019: Assessment Framework and Results*, June 2019

Data sharing agreements and data service level agreements (data SLAs) may be used to manage a chained set of data attestations to support the overall data attestation of the DFAST 14A report to the regulators (Figure 10.3).

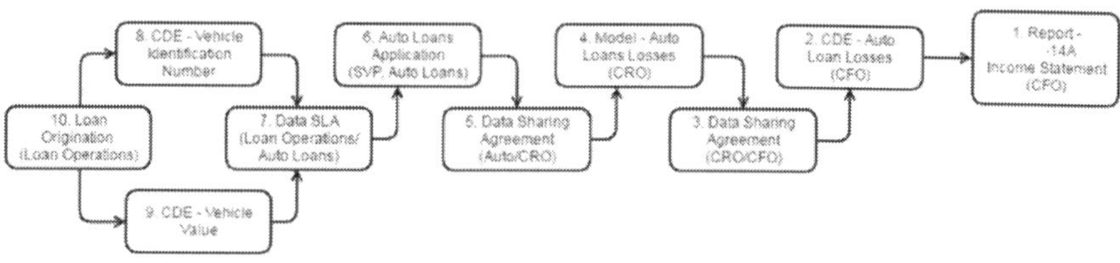

Figure 10.3: Data sharing agreements chained together to support data attestation for DFAST 14A report

Each component in the traceability diagram is explained in Table 10.3.

Current Expected Credit Loss

On June 16, 2016, the U.S. Financial Accounting Standards Board (FASB) completed its Financial Instruments–Credit Losses project by issuing Accounting Standards Update No. 2016-13, *Financial Instruments–Credit Losses (Topic 326)*. The new guidance requires organizations to measure all expected credit losses for financial instruments held at the reporting date based on historical experience, current conditions, and reasonable and supportable forecasts.

Before CECL, Generally Accepted Accounting Principles (GAAP) required an "incurred loss" methodology for recognizing credit losses that delayed recognition until it was probable a loss had been incurred. This model had been criticized for restricting an organization's ability to record credit losses that were expected but did not yet meet the "probable" threshold. The global financial crisis underscored those concerns. In the lead-up to the financial crisis, financial statement users were making estimates of expected credit losses using forward-looking information and devaluing financial institutions before accounting losses were recognized. This situation highlighted that the information needs of users differed from what GAAP then required. Similarly, preparers expressed frustration during this period because they could not record credit losses that they were expecting due to the fact that the probable threshold had not been met.[37]

Table 10.3: Chaining of data sharing agreements and data SLAs to support data attestation

Artifact	Type	Attester to report, CDE, model, application, or signatory to data sharing agreement or data SLA
1. OCC DFAST 14A Schedule A.1.a – Income Statement	Report	Chief Financial Officer
2. Losses Associated with Auto Loans Held for Investment at Amortized Cost (Line Item 31 in report)	CDE	Chief Financial Officer
3. Sharing of auto loan risk model by CRO with CFO	Data sharing agreement	Chief Risk Officer (Data Producer) Chief Financial Officer (Data Consumer)
4. Auto loan loss risk model	Model	Chief Risk Officer
5. Sharing of auto loan data by auto loans division with CRO	Data sharing agreement	Senior Vice President of Auto Loans (Data Producer) CRO (Data Consumer)
6. Auto loan application	Application	Senior Vice President of Auto Loans (Data Executive of the auto loans data category)
7. Bulk data movement from loan origination system to auto loan application	Data service level agreement with acceptable thresholds for missing VINs and vehicle value	Senior Vice President of Loan Operations (Data Producer) Senior Vice President of Auto Loans (Data Consumer)
8. Vehicle Identification Number (VIN)	CDE	Senior Vice President of Loan Operations
9. Vehicle Value	CDE	Senior Vice President of Loan Operations
10. Loan origination system	Application	Senior Vice President of Loan Operations

[37] Financial Accounting Standards Board, "Credit Losses," https://www.fasb.org/creditlosses

To that end, the new CECL guidance:

- Eliminates the probable initial recognition threshold in current GAAP and, instead, reflects an organization's current estimate of all expected credit losses over the contractual term of its financial assets
- Broadens the information that an entity can consider when measuring credit losses to include forward-looking information
- Increases usefulness of the financial statements by requiring timely inclusion of forecasted information in forming expectations of credit losses
- Increases comparability of purchased financial assets with credit deterioration (PCD assets) with other purchased assets that do not have credit deterioration as well as originated assets because credit losses that are expected will be recorded through an allowance for credit losses for all assets
- Increases users' understanding of underwriting standards and credit quality trends by requiring additional information about credit quality indicators by year of origination (vintage)
- For available-for-sale debt securities, aligns the income statement recognition of credit losses with the reporting period in which changes occur by recording credit losses (and subsequent changes in credit losses) through an allowance rather than a write-down

CECL affects organizations that hold financial assets and net investments in leases that are not accounted for at fair value with changes in fair value reported in net income.

The new guidance affects loans, debt securities, trade receivables, net investments in leases, off-balance-sheet credit exposures, reinsurance receivables, and any other financial assets not excluded from the scope that have the contractual right to receive cash.

Table 10.4 reviews sample CDEs for CECL.

Table 10.4: CDEs for CECL compliance

Critical data element	Definition
1. Purchased Financial Assets with Credit Deterioration (PCD)	Acquired individual financial assets (or acquired groups of financial assets with similar risk characteristics) that as of the date of acquisition have experienced a more-than-insignificant deterioration in credit quality since origination, as determined by an acquirer's assessment.
2. Amortized Cost Basis	The amount at which a financing receivable or investment is originated or acquired, adjusted for applicable accrued interest, accretion, or amortization of premium, discount, and net deferred fees or costs, collection of cash, previous other-than-temporary impairments recognized in earnings (less any cumulative-effect adjustments), write-offs, foreign exchange, and fair value hedge accounting adjustments.
3. Estimated Paydown	Expected payments in the future periods until the pool is expected to fully pay off. (Management will need to estimate the future paydowns, which include the scheduled payments plus prepayments.)
4. Portfolio Segment	The level at which an entity develops and documents a systematic methodology to determine its allowance for credit losses.
5. Credit Score	A numerical expression based on a level analysis of a person's credit files, to represent the creditworthiness of an individual. A credit score is based primarily on a credit report, information typically sourced from credit bureaus.
6. Loan Type	Type of loan (secured or unsecured).
7. Debt-to-Value Ratio	The debt divided by the sum of the debt and the equity.
8. Probability of Default (PD)	A financial term describing the likelihood of a default over a particular time horizon.
9. GL Account Identifier	A unique identification number for general ledger account.

Table 10.5 describes sample data quality rules for CECL.

Table 10.5: Data quality rules for CECL compliance

Critical data element	Data quality rule
1. Loan Type	If loan type is secured, then the value of collateral cannot be null
2. Loan Type	If loan type is unsecured, then the value of collateral should be null
3. Probability of Default (PD)	If PD is 1, then loan loss provision should be 100 percent of loan outstanding balance

Figure 10.4 shows the CECL CDEs in YourDataConnect.

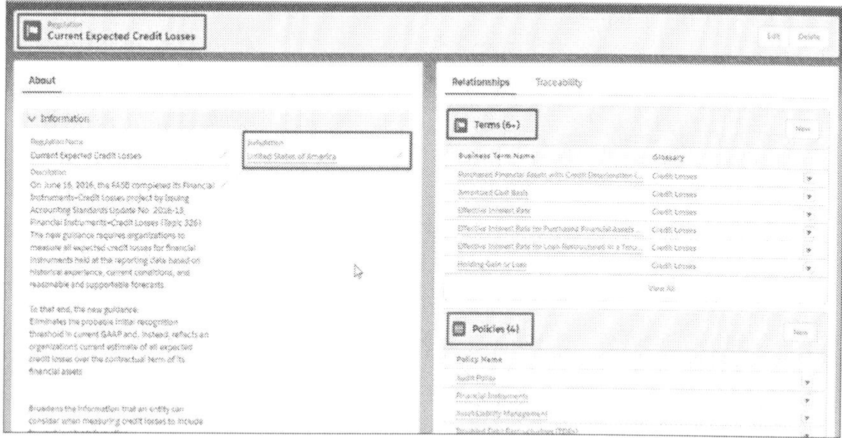

Figure 10.4: CECL CDEs in YourDataConnect

Figure 10.5 shows the mapping of the *GL Account ID cannot be null* business rule to the *GL Account Identifier* in YourDataConnect.

Office of Foreign Assets Control

The Office of Terrorism and Financial Intelligence (TFI), formed in 2004, is an agency of the United States Department of the Treasury. TFI works to reduce the use of the financial system for illicit activities by

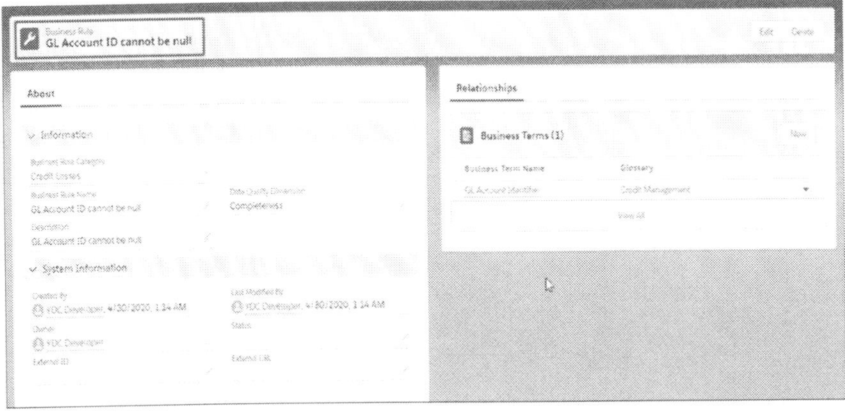

Figure 10.5: Mapping of business rule to CDE in YourDataConnect

terrorists (groups and state-sponsored), money launderers, drug cartels, and other national security threats.[38]

TFI is overseen by the Under Secretary of the Treasury for Terrorism and Financial Intelligence and oversees the following:

- Office of Terrorist Financing and Financial Crimes
- Office of Intelligence and Analysis
- Office of Foreign Assets Control (OFAC)
- Financial Crimes Enforcement Network (FinCEN)
- Treasury Executive Office for Asset Forfeiture

In addition to the Trading with the Enemy Act and the various national emergencies currently in effect, OFAC derives its authority from a variety of U.S. federal laws regarding embargoes and economic sanctions.

In enforcing economic sanctions, OFAC acts to prevent "prohibited transactions," which are described by OFAC as "trade or financial transactions and other dealings in which U.S. persons may not engage unless authorized by OFAC or expressly exempted by statute." OFAC has the authority to grant exemptions to prohibitions on such transactions, either by issuing a general license for certain categories of transactions or by specific licenses issued on a case-by-case basis. OFAC administers and enforces economic sanctions programs against countries, businesses,

[38] Wikipedia, "Office of Terrorism and Financial Intelligence," https://en.wikipedia.org/wiki/Office_of_Terrorism_and_Financial_Intelligence

or groups of individuals, using the blocking of assets and trade restrictions to accomplish foreign policy and national security goals.

Under the International Emergency Economic Powers Act (IEEPA), the U.S. president is empowered during national emergencies to block the removal of foreign assets under the jurisdiction of the United States. OFAC executes that mandate by issuing regulations that direct financial institutions accordingly.

OFAC publishes a list of Sectoral Sanctions Identifications (SSI), which lists persons, companies, and entities in sectors of the Russian economy (especially energy, finance, and armaments), prohibiting certain types of activity with these individuals or entities by U.S. persons, wherever located. This list is maintained following the issuance of Executive Order 13662–"Blocking Property of Additional Persons Contributing to the Situation in Ukraine" on March 20, 2014, in accordance with 79 FR 16167.

As part of its enforcement efforts, OFAC publishes a list of individuals and companies owned or controlled by, or acting for or on behalf of, targeted countries. It also lists individuals, groups, and entities, such as terrorists and narcotics traffickers designated under programs that are not country specific. Collectively, such individuals and companies are called "Specially Designated Nationals" (SDNs). Their assets are blocked, and U.S. persons are generally prohibited from dealing with them.[39]

Because data management for OFAC focuses on maintaining trustworthy data regarding the organization's customers, many of the CDEs and data quality rules for BSA/AML also apply.

Financial Crimes Enforcement Network

The Financial Crimes Enforcement Network (FinCEN) is a bureau of the U.S. Department of the Treasury that collects and analyzes information about financial transactions in order to combat domestic and international money laundering, terrorist financing, and other financial crimes.

FinCEN shares information with dozens of intelligence agencies, including the Bureau of Alcohol, Tobacco, and Firearms, the Drug Enforcement Administration, the Federal Bureau of Investigation, the U.S. Secret Service, the Internal Revenue Service, the Customs Service, and the U.S. Postal Inspection Service.

---

[39] Wikipedia, "Office of Foreign Assets Control," https://en.wikipedia.org/wiki/Office_of_Foreign_Assets_Control

FinCen is involved with several programs:

- *314 Program of the USA Patriot Act*—The 2001 USA PATRIOT Act required the Secretary of the Treasury to create a secure network for the transmission of information to enforce the relevant regulations. FinCEN's regulations under Section 314(a) enable federal law enforcement agencies, through FinCEN, to reach out to more than 45,000 points of contact at more than 27,000 financial institutions to locate accounts and transactions of persons that may be involved in terrorist financing and/or money laundering. A web interface allows the person(s) designated in §314(a)(3)(A) to register and transmit information to FinCEN. The partnership between the financial community and law enforcement allows disparate bits of information to be identified, centralized, and rapidly evaluated.
- *Hawala*—As early as 2003, FinCEN disseminated information on "informal value transfer systems" (IVTS), including hawala, a network of people receiving money for the purpose of making the funds payable to a third party in another geographic location, generally taking place outside the conventional banking system through non-bank financial institutions or other business entities whose primary business activity may not be the transmission of money.
- *Virtual currencies such as Bitcoin*—In July 2011, FinCEN added "other value that substitutes for currency" to its definition of money services businesses in preparation for adapting the respective rule to virtual currencies. On March 18, 2013, it issued guidance regarding virtual currencies, according to which exchangers and administrators, but not users of convertible virtual currency, are considered money transmitters, and must comply with rules to prevent money laundering, terrorist financing and other forms of financial crime, by recordkeeping, reporting, and registering with FinCEN.

Because data management for FinCEN focuses on maintaining trustworthy data regarding the organization's customers, many of the CDEs and data quality rules for BSA/AML also apply.

Summary

Financial services companies have to comply with several regulations, many of which are data-intensive from a compliance perspective. In the United States, these regulations include BSA/AML, CCAR, CECL, DFAST, FinCEN, and OFAC.

11

Life Sciences Regulations

Life sciences firms need to comply with several industry-specific, data-intensive regulations, including the following:

- Identification of Medicinal Products (IDMP)
- European Union Medical Device Regulation (MDR)
- United States Food and Drug Administration Unique Device Identification System final rule (UDI Rule)

Identification of Medicinal Products

Identification of Medicinal Products (IDMP) is a suite of five standards developed within the International Organization for Standardization (ISO). These standards provide an internationally accepted framework to uniquely identify and describe medicinal products with consistent documentation, coding, and exchange of product information between global regulators, manufacturers, suppliers, and distributors. The IDMP suite of standards are a result of a need to standardize the definition of medicinal product and substance information to facilitate the unique identification and exchange of such information in the context of pharmacovigilance.[40]

The European Medicines Agency (EMA) is in the process of implementing the IDMP standards in a phased program based on the four domains of master data in pharmaceutical regulatory processes: substance, product, organization, and referential (SPOR) master data.

---

[40] U.S. Food and Drug Administration, "Identification of Medicinal Products (IDMP)," https://www.fda.gov/industry/fda-resources-data-standards/identification-medicinal-products-idmp

The five standards provide data elements and structures to uniquely identify and exchange information about:

- Substances (ISO 11238)
- Pharmaceutical dose forms, units of presentation, routes of administration, and packaging (ISO 11239)
- Units of measurement (ISO 11240)
- Regulated pharmaceutical product information (ISO 11616)
- Regulated medicinal product information (ISO 11615)

These standards cover the following aspects to describe a medicinal product for human use:

- Medicinal product name
- Ingredient substances
- Pharmaceutical product (route of administration, strength)
- Marketing authorization
- Clinical particulars
- Packaging
- Manufacturing

ISO IDMP covers the entire medicinal product lifecycle, including products in development, investigational products, products under evaluation, and authorized products. Although ISO IDMP standards relate to human medicinal products, SPOR applies to both human and veterinary domains.[41]

Figure 11.1 shows product information in YourDataConnect™. This information is approved using the rich workflows in YourDataConnect.

The information is then sent to Informatica® Reference 360 via the pre-built integration with YourDataConnect (Figure 11.2).

Figure 11.3 shows pharmaceutical data in Microsoft® Excel®.

---

[41] European Medicines Agency, "Data on Medicines (ISO IDMP Standards): Overview," https://www.ema.europa.eu/en/human-regulatory/overview/data-medicines-iso-idmp-standards-overview

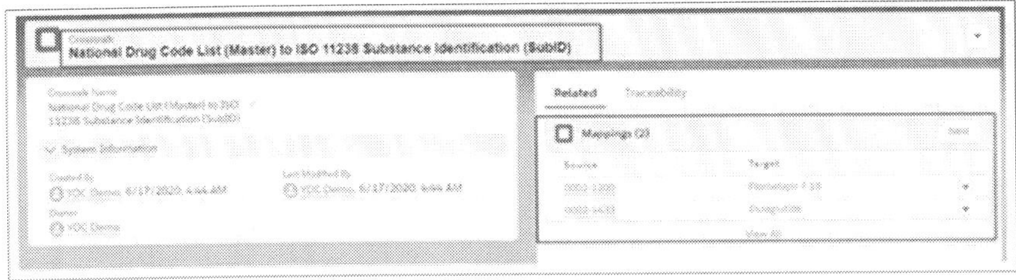

Figure 11.1: Product information in YourDataConnect™

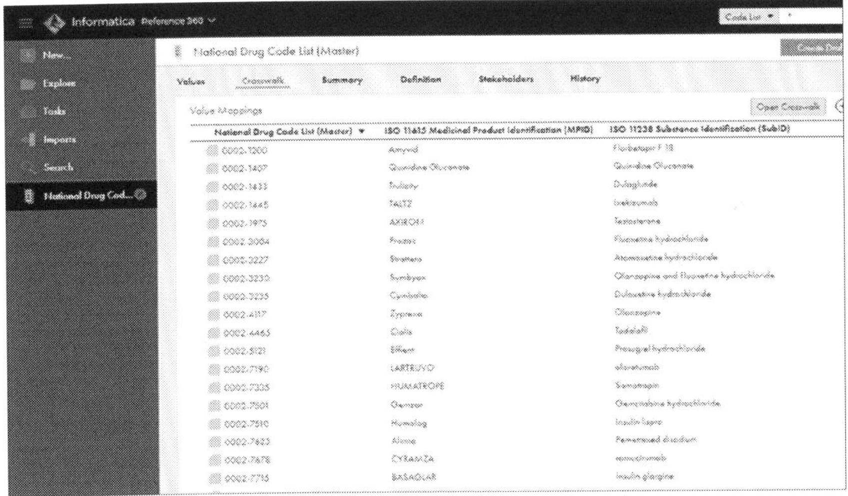

Figure 11.2: Crosswalks in Informatica® Reference 360

Figure 11.3: Pharmaceutical data in Microsoft® Excel®

Figure 11.4 shows the information loaded into Amazon® Redshift™.

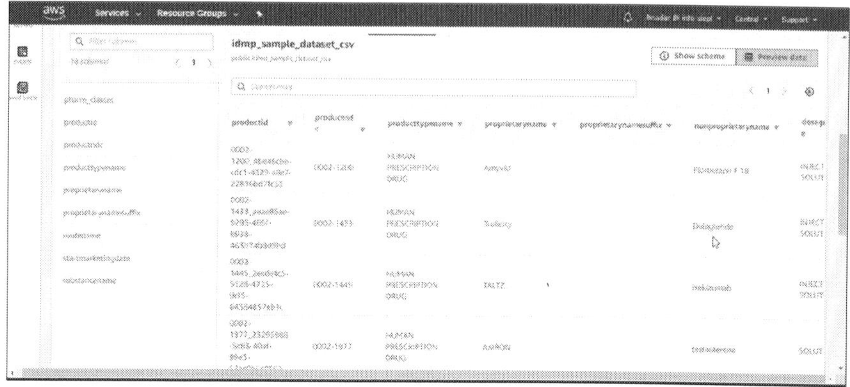

Figure 11.4: Pharmaceutical information loaded into Amazon® Redshift®

Figure 11.5 shows a basic Tableau® report with the same underlying information.

Medical products report

Proprietaryname	Productndc	Producttypename	Substancename	Dosageformname	Applicationnu..
ACCURETIC	0071-0220	HUMAN PRESCRIPTION D..	QUINAPRIL HYDROCHLOR..	TABLET, FILM COATED	NDA020125
	0071-0222	HUMAN PRESCRIPTION D..	QUINAPRIL HYDROCHLOR..	TABLET, FILM COATED	NDA020125
	0071-0223	HUMAN PRESCRIPTION D..	QUINAPRIL HYDROCHLOR..	TABLET, FILM COATED	NDA020125
ACULAR LS	0023-8277	HUMAN PRESCRIPTION D..	KETOROLAC TROMETHAM..	SOLUTION/ DROPS	NDA021528
ACUVAIL	0023-3507	HUMAN PRESCRIPTION D..	KETOROLAC TROMETHAM..	SOLUTION/ DROPS	NDA022427
ACZONE	0023-3670	HUMAN PRESCRIPTION D..	DAPSONE	GEL	NDA021794
ACZONE (dapsone) Gel, 7..	0023-5206	HUMAN PRESCRIPTION D..	DAPSONE	GEL	NDA207154
ALDACTAZIDE	0025-1011	HUMAN PRESCRIPTION D..	SPIRONOLACTONE; HYDR..	TABLET, FILM COATED	NDA012616
	0025-1021	HUMAN PRESCRIPTION D..	SPIRONOLACTONE; HYDR..	TABLET, FILM COATED	NDA012616
ALOCRIL	0023-8842	HUMAN PRESCRIPTION D..	NEDOCROMIL SODIUM	SOLUTION/ DROPS	NDA021009
ALOMIDE	0065-0345	HUMAN PRESCRIPTION D..	LODOXAMIDE TROMETHA..	SOLUTION/ DROPS	NDA020191
ALPHAGAN P	0023-9177	HUMAN PRESCRIPTION D..	BRIMONIDINE TARTRATE	SOLUTION/ DROPS	NDA021262
	0023-9321	HUMAN PRESCRIPTION D..	BRIMONIDINE TARTRATE	SOLUTION/ DROPS	NDA021770
AMARYL	0039-0221	HUMAN PRESCRIPTION D..	GLIMEPIRIDE	TABLET	NDA020496
	0039-0222	HUMAN PRESCRIPTION D..	GLIMEPIRIDE	TABLET	NDA020496
	0039-0223	HUMAN PRESCRIPTION D..	GLIMEPIRIDE	TABLET	NDA020496
ARGATROBAN	0007-4407	HUMAN PRESCRIPTION D..	ARGATROBAN	INJECTION, SOLUTION	NDA020883
ARRANON	0007-4401	HUMAN PRESCRIPTION D..	NELARABINE	INJECTION	NDA021877
ARTHROTEC	0025-1411	HUMAN PRESCRIPTION D..	DICLOFENAC SODIUM; MI..	TABLET, FILM COATED	NDA020607
	0025-1421	HUMAN PRESCRIPTION D..	DICLOFENAC SODIUM; MI..	TABLET, FILM COATED	NDA020607
ARZERRA	0078-0669	HUMAN PRESCRIPTION D..	OFATUMUMAB	INJECTION, SOLUTION	BLA125326
	0078-0690	HUMAN PRESCRIPTION D..	OFATUMUMAB	INJECTION, SOLUTION	BLA125326
ASMANEX	0085-1341	HUMAN PRESCRIPTION D..	MOMETASONE FUROATE	INHALANT	NDA021067
	0085-1461	HUMAN PRESCRIPTION D..	MOMETASONE FUROATE	INHALANT	NDA021067
AVAGE	0023-9236	HUMAN PRESCRIPTION D..	TAZAROTENE	CREAM	NDA021184
AVC	0037-6631	HUMAN PRESCRIPTION D..	SULFANILAMIDE	CREAM	NDA006530
AXIRON	0002-1975	HUMAN PRESCRIPTION D..	TESTOSTERONE	SOLUTION	NDA022504
	0002-1977	HUMAN PRESCRIPTION D..	TESTOSTERONE	SOLUTION	NDA022504
AZACTAM	0003-2230	HUMAN PRESCRIPTION D..	AZTREONAM	INJECTION, SOLUTION	NDA050632
	0003-2240	HUMAN PRESCRIPTION D..	AZTREONAM	INJECTION, SOLUTION	NDA050632

Figure 11.5: Tableau® report with pharmaceutical information

Figure 11.6 shows the data lineage from Tableau to Amazon Redshift displayed in YourDataConnect.

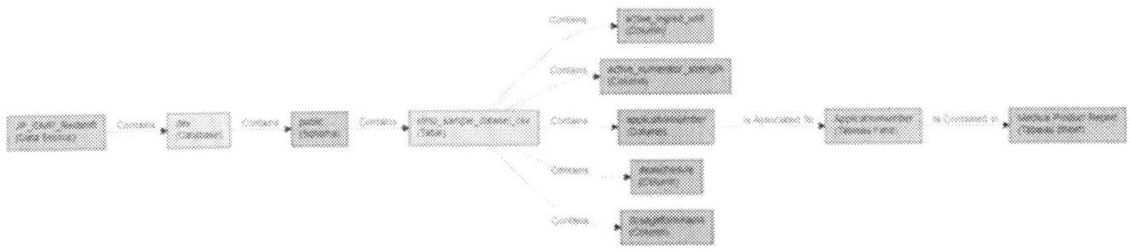

Figure 11.6: Data lineage from Tableau to Amazon Redshift in YourDataConnect

European Union Medical Device Regulation

Effective May 2021, the MDR lays down rules concerning the placing on the market, making available on the market, or putting into service medical devices for human use and accessories for such devices in the European Union. The MDR also applies to clinical investigations concerning such medical devices and accessories conducted in the European Union.

Among many requirements, the MDR requires consistent, high-quality product master data relating to medical devices.

Table 11.1 reviews sample CDEs for MDR.[42]

Table 11.1: CDEs for MDR compliance

Critical data element	Definition
1. Basic UDI-DI	The Basic UDI-DI (Unique Device Identifier–Device Identifier) is the primary identifier of a device model. It is the DI assigned at the level of the device unit of use. It is the main key for records in the UDI database and is referenced in relevant certificates and EU declarations of conformity.
2. Unit of Use UDI-DI	The Unit of Use UDI-DI serves to associate the use of a device with a patient in instances in which a UDI is not labeled on the individual device at the level of its unit of use; for example, in the event of several units of the same device being packaged together. *Continued*

[42] Annex VI of the European Union Medical Device Regulation

Table 11.1: CDEs for MDR compliance *(continued)*	
Critical data element	**Definition**
3. UDI-PI	The Production Identifier is a conditional, variable part of the UDI, not required for Class I, that includes 1) lot, batch, or serial number, 2) expiration date or manufacture date, and 3) the distinct identification code for Human Cell and Tissue Products (HCT/P) when regulated as a device.
4. UDI-DI	The UDI-DI is a unique numeric or alphanumeric code that is specific to a model of device and that is also used as the access key to information stored in the EUDAMED database within the EU.
5. GTIN	Global Trade Item Number.
6. UOM	Unit of Measure.

Table 11.2 describes sample data quality rules for MDR.

Table 11.2: Data quality rules for MDR compliance	
Critical data element	**Data quality rule**
1. Product Description	Product description should not be null
2. Product Description	Product description should not contain special characters (*, $, #)
3. Product Description	Product description should not contain "Do Not Use"

United States Food and Drug Administration UDI Final Rule

The United States FDA established the unique device identification system to adequately identify medical devices sold in the United States from manufacturing through distribution to patient use. The Unique Device Identification System final rule (UDI Rule) requires device labelers to include a UDI on device labels and packages and to submit device information to the Global Unique Device Identification Database (GUDID). Compliance with this rule also requires consistent product master data. However, there are some differences in data formats between the FDA and the MDR.

Summary

Life sciences firms need to comply with several industry-specific, data-intensive regulations, including IDMP, EU MDR, and the UDI Rule. YourDataConnect supports the management of pharmaceutical data.

12

Data Marketplace

A data marketplace is an online catalog of datasets that allows for the internal or external monetization of data. A data marketplace allows organizations to list curated data sets and other reusable data assets such as business intelligence (BI) reports or representational state transfer (REST) application programming interfaces (APIs). Lines of business can register assets they own in the marketplace so that other users can browse them and request access. The other users could be from within the dataset owner's line of business, another line of business, or a third-party, such as a partner, customer, or regulator.

Data Marketplace Personas

There are three main personas in the YourDataConnect™ data marketplace:

- *Publisher*—This persona represents a user that registers assets in the marketplace for other users to request.
- *Administrator*—This persona represents users who administer the marketplace. The Administrator persona reviews new datasets that are registered; upon approval, the datasets are listed on the marketplace. This persona also reviews dataset requests, which can be shared with the subscriber upon approval.
- *Subscriber*—This persona represents a user who is browsing the marketplace for datasets and subscribing to one of interest.

Publisher Persona

Publishers can register two types of datasets in the marketplace: internal or external.

Internal datasets, such as *Employee Emails*, are generated within the organization by a particular line of business. Each dataset is described by attributes such as *Name*, *Description*, *Owner Cost Center*, *Data Steward*, *Contains PII*, *Record Type*, *Price*, *Status*, and *Frequency* as seen in Figure 12.1.

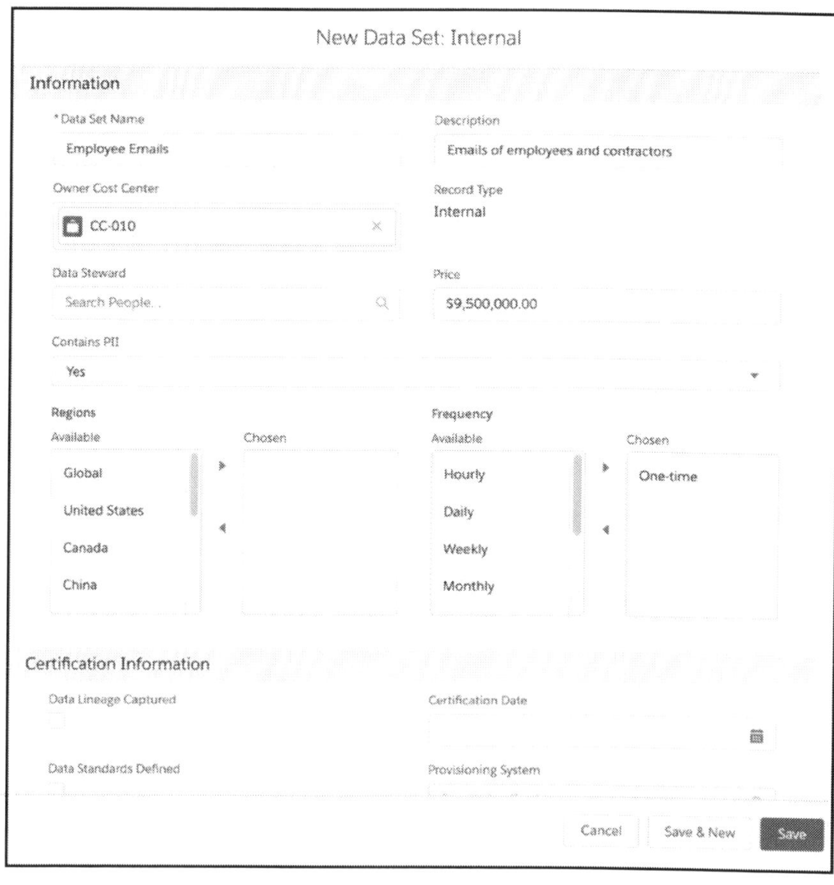

Figure 12.1: Internal Employee Emails dataset in YourDataConnect™

External datasets are sourced from a third-party provider. In addition to the fields shown in Figure 12.1, fields such as *External Provider* and *Price Paid to External Provider* are captured for external datasets (Figure 12.2).

Figure 12.2: External datasets contain provider information in YourDataConnect

Administrator Persona

After the publisher registers an internal dataset or an external dataset in YourDataConnect, the request goes through a series of approvals. These approval steps are customizable. By default, the approval steps include:

- Finance Approval
- Privacy Approval
- Legal Approval

Subscriber Persona

Once final approval is complete, the status of the dataset changes to *Approved*, and the dataset appears in the YourDataConnect marketplace user interface so that subscribers can request access (Figure 12.3).

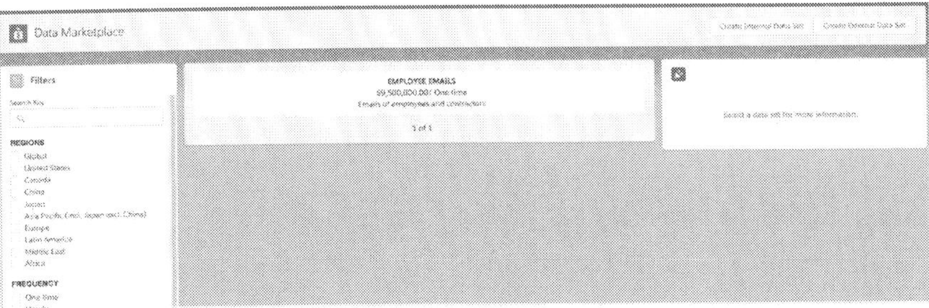

Figure 12.3: Employee emails appear in the YourDataConnect marketplace user interface

When an internal user submits a request to subscribe to a particular dataset, the requestor specifies the cost center as well as the purpose of the request (Figure 12.4).

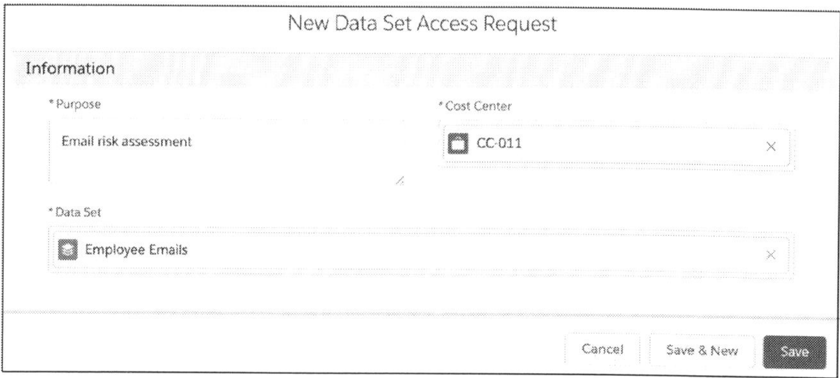

Figure 12.4: New dataset access request in YourDataConnect

If the data owner approves the request, a cross-charge record is created, as shown in Figure 12.5.

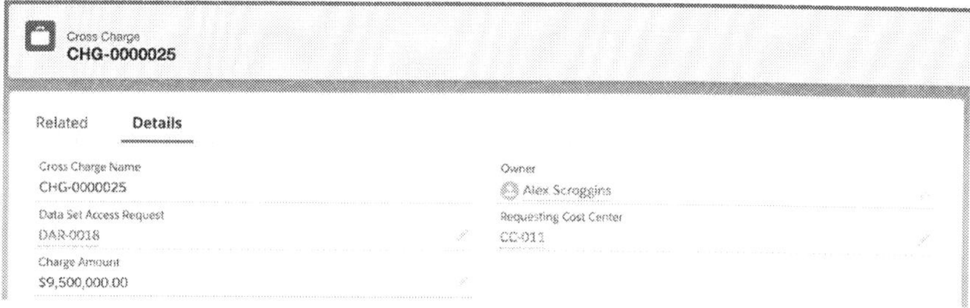

Figure 12.5: Cross-charge request in YourDataConnect

Regulatory Compliance

Datasets may be related to relevant regulations, as shown in Figure 12.6. Here, the *Employee Emails* dataset is related to CCPA and GDPR. Also shown in the figure are the relevant data access requests for this dataset. This information establishes a record of processing activities as mandated by these regulations (for example, Article 30 of the GDPR).

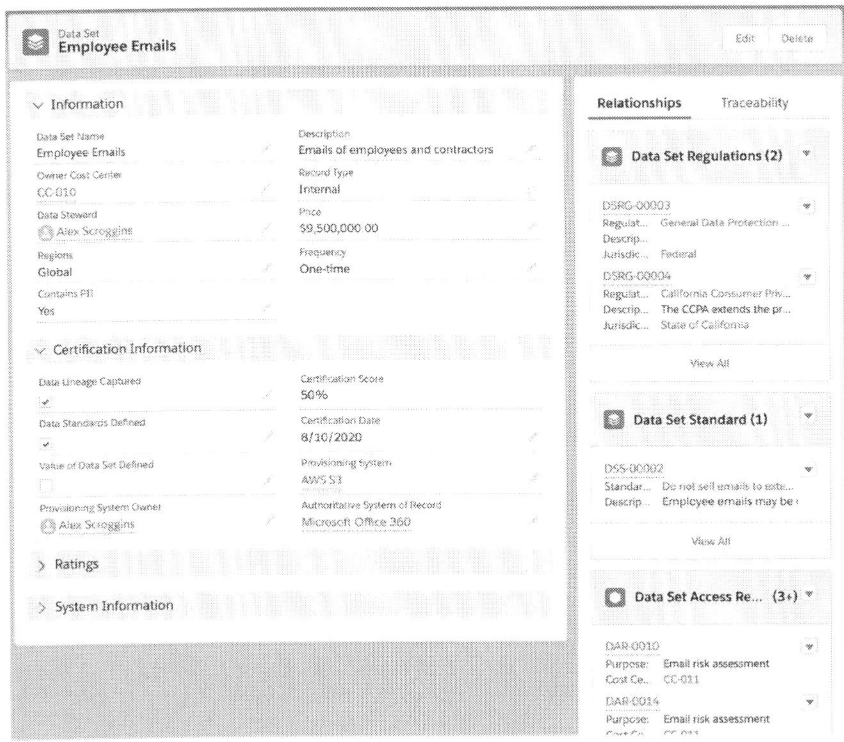

Figure 12.6: Employee Emails dataset in YourDataConnect is related to regulations and access requests

Internal Data Sharing

In addition to curated data assets, YourDataConnect may be used to monetize the ad hoc sharing of data. Users may not always find datasets that meet their needs when using the data marketplace. For this scenario, YourDataConnect provides a workflow where users can describe the data they need, submit the request for approvals, gain access upon final approval, and have cross charges recorded, if applicable. As shown in Figure 12.7, users can indicate whether or not they know the location of the requested data. The figure shows a user specifying that they do not know where the requested data is located.

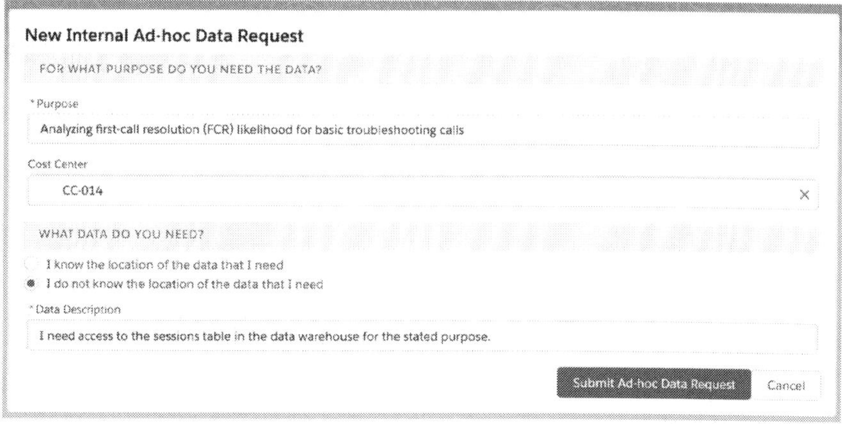

New Internal Ad-hoc Data Request

FOR WHAT PURPOSE DO YOU NEED THE DATA?

* Purpose

Analyzing first-call resolution (FCR) likelihood for basic troubleshooting calls

Cost Center

CC-014

WHAT DATA DO YOU NEED?

( ) I know the location of the data that I need

(•) I do not know the location of the data that I need

* Data Description

I need access to the sessions table in the data warehouse for the stated purpose.

Submit Ad-hoc Data Request | Cancel

Figure 12.7: New internal ad hoc sharing request in YourDataConnect where the user does not know the location of the data they need

Figure 12.8 shows a case where a user knows the location of the requested data. In this case, the user is required to select one or more data assets, such as tables or columns. The metadata for the associated tables and columns has been pre-scanned using YourDataConnect's data catalog function.

New Internal Ad-hoc Data Request

FOR WHAT PURPOSE DO YOU NEED THE DATA?

* Purpose

Analyzing first-call resolution (FCR) likelihood for basic troubleshooting calls

Cost Center

CC-014

WHAT DATA DO YOU NEED?

(•) I know the location of the data that I need

( ) I do not know the location of the data that I need

Data to Share

Session

DEV.PUBLIC.FACT_SESSIONS.SESSION_AGENT_ID
Column • DEV.PUBLIC.FACT_SESSIONS.SESSION_AGENT_ID

DEV.PUBLIC.FACT_SESSIONS.SESSION_ENDED_AT
Column • DEV.PUBLIC.FACT_SESSIONS.SESSION_ENDED_AT

DEV.PUBLIC.FACT_SESSIONS.SESSION_STARTED_AT
Column • DEV.PUBLIC.FACT_SESSIONS.SESSION_STARTED_AT

FACT_SESSIONS
Table • FACT_SESSIONS

Figure 12.8: New internal ad hoc sharing request in YourDataConnect where the user knows the location of the data they need

External Data Sharing

YourDataConnect also supports workflows where the organization has a contract involving data sharing with a third party. Figure 12.9 shows a form for submitting an ad hoc data sharing request on behalf of the third-party.

YourDataConnect allows this form to be configured to pull the *External Party* list from customer relationship management (CRM), master data management (MDM), or enterprise resource planning (ERP) software. In this case, the External Party list is integrated with Salesforce® Sales Cloud.

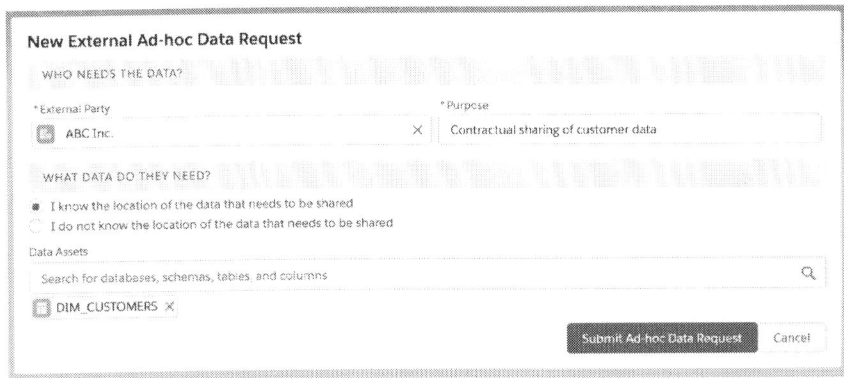

Figure 12.9: New external ad hoc sharing request in YourDataConnect where the user knows the location of the data they need

Data Valuation

YourDataConnect supports business case functionality to help data owners value their data. This data valuation capability allows data owners to monetize their data either internally or externally via the data marketplace. Figure 12.10 shows a collection of inputs requested from a user to define the value per record of the customer date of birth.

Business Cases > Improve DOB Data Quality

Business Case Inputs

11 items • Sorted by Variable Order • Updated a few seconds ago

	Variable Order	Variable Name	Variable Description	Value	Automated/Manual
1	1	A	Number of customers in the retail bank	10,000,000	Manual
2	2	B	Estimated percentage of customer records with inaccurate dates of birth	5%	Manual
3	3	C	Estimate number of retail banking customers with inaccurate dates of birth	500,000	Automated
4	4	D	Annual percentage of customers who call the bank with a request to buy anothe...	10%	Manual
5	5	E	Average dropout rate associated with customers who have to visit a branch to co...	50%	Manual
6	6	F	Estimated number of annual cross-sell opportunities that are lost because of dr...	25,000	Automated
7	7	G	Average value of product that is cross-sold to existing customers	$20,000.00	Manual
8	8	H	Average operating margin on products that are cross-sold to existing customers	5%	Manual
9	9	I	Potential increase in annual operating margin by improving the quality of dates ...	$25,000,000.00	Automated
10	10	J	Date of Birth CDE	Customer Date of Birth	Manual
11	11	K	Date of Birth CDE Value per Record	$50.00	Automated

Figure 12.10: Business case inputs for customer date of birth

Differential Rules of Visibility

YourDataConnect also supports differential rules of visibility so that different roles can view different datasets within a data catalog. For example, the commodities trading group at a large hedge fund can view weather-related datasets in YourDataConnect (Figure 12.11).

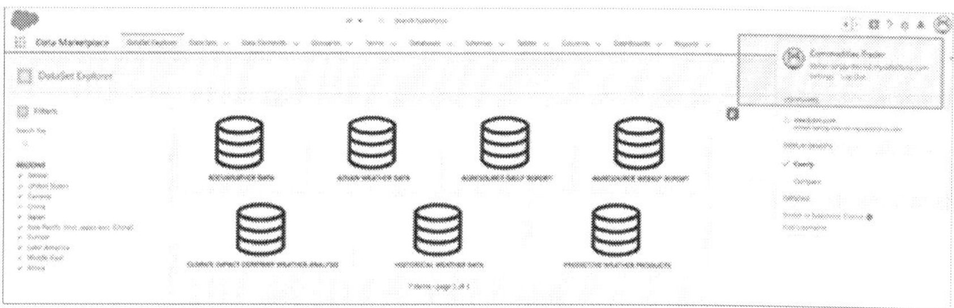

Figure 12.11: Commodities trading group can view weather-related datasets in YourDataConnect

Similarly, the equities trading group can view a market-related dataset in YourDataConnect (Figure 12.12).

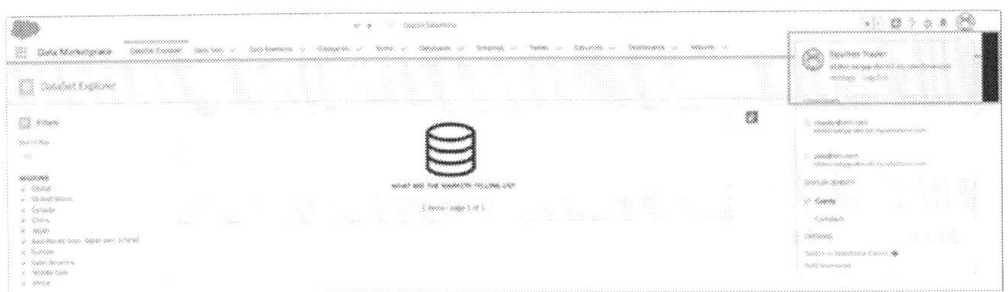

Figure 12.12: Equities trading group can view market-related datasets in YourDataConnect

Finally, only an *Admin* user from the data management team can view certain attributes, such as the *Price* paid for a dataset (Figure 12.13).

Figure 12.13: Only Admin users can view the Price attribute of a dataset in YourDataConnect

Summary

A data marketplace is an online catalog of datasets that allows for the internal or external monetization of data. Lines of business can register assets they own in the marketplace so that other users can browse them and request access. The other users could be from within the dataset owner's line of business, another line of business, or a third-party such as a partner, customer, or regulator. Data marketplaces should support publisher, administrator, and subscriber personas. Finally, data marketplaces should support internal and external data sharing, regulatory compliance, data valuation, and differential rules of visibility.

13

YourDataConnect Overview

YourDataConnect™ is the industry's first software-as-a-service (SaaS) data monetization platform to help organizations capture financial benefits by growing revenues, reducing costs, and managing risk.

To achieve this, business cases identified using the methodology presented earlier in this book are entered into the YourDataConnect platform. Once entered, an overall estimated value is calculated for the business case. Next, integration and automation assist with realizing that value. Finally, the realized benefits of data monetization are certified by finance.

A number of features exist in YourDataConnect to manage the lifecycle of a business case. These features include the following, which are discussed in detail in this chapter:

- Dashboards for measuring data monetization status and results
- Workflows for managing human tasks around data monetization, including approval processes
- Business glossary for understanding the business context of data monetization
- Data catalog for capturing the technical data assets relevant to data monetization
- Data privacy for respecting and complying with data privacy rights by jurisdiction in the context of data monetization
- Reference data management for ensuring that data relevant to business cases is translatable across different contexts
- Regulatory compliance for adhering to regulatory requirements applicable to data monetization business cases

Data Monetization Dashboard

Figure 13.1 shows an example of the data monetization dashboard in YourDataConnect. This dashboard summarizes the business cases that have been created and shows their estimated and potential realizable values.

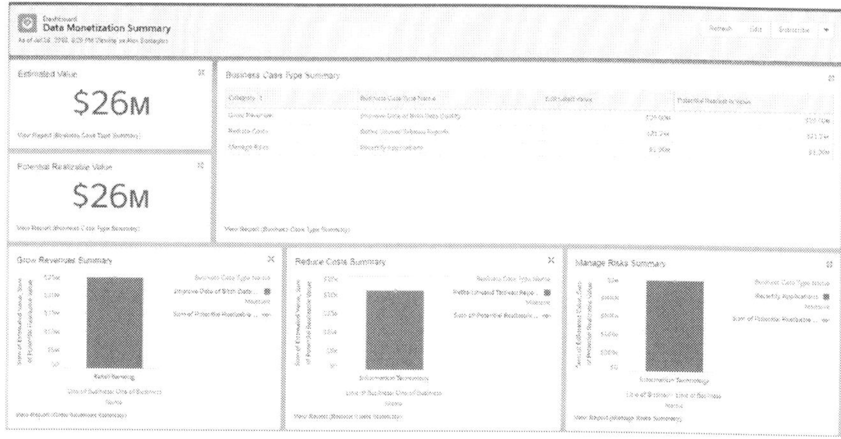

Figure 13.1: Data monetization dashboard in YourDataConnect™

Dashboard

YourDataConnect contains several dashboards, and new dashboards can be created without the need to write code. A sample out-of-the-box dashboard is shown in Figure 13.2. This dashboard shows the percentage of business terms that have been mapped to columns (and vice versa).

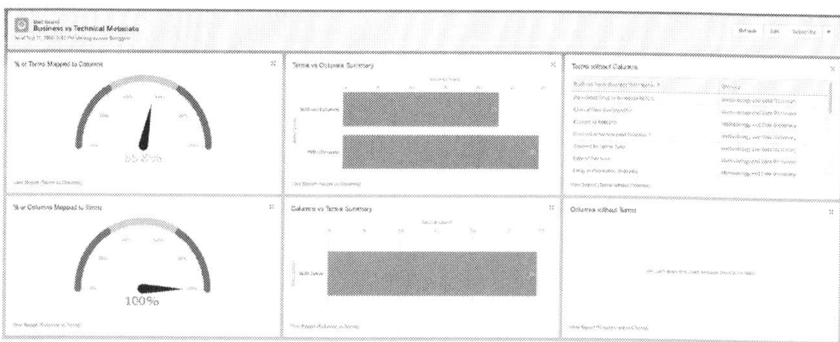

Figure 13.2: Business vs. technical metadata dashboard in YourDataConnect

Figure 13.3 shows an example of another dashboard. This dashboard shows a summary of Tableau® reports and dashboards that can be considered for retirement because they have not been used in the past 90 days.

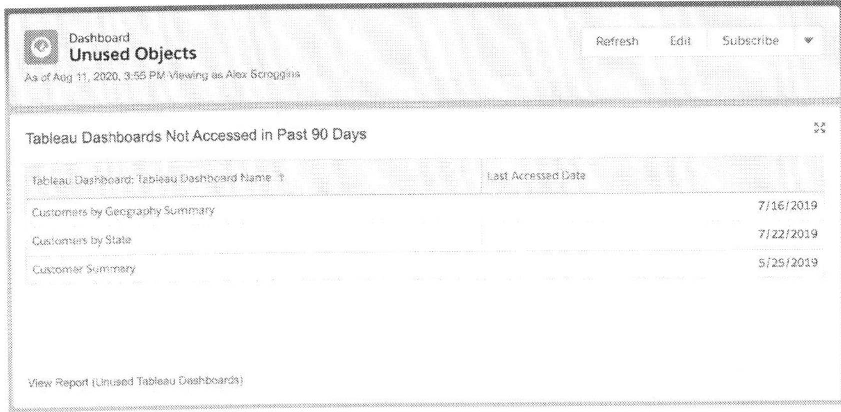

Figure 13.3: Unused Tableau® objects dashboard in YourDataConnect

Business Glossary

The business glossary allows organizations to define a collection of business terms and their definitions. A sample glossary for customer-related terms and their definitions is shown in Figure 13.4.

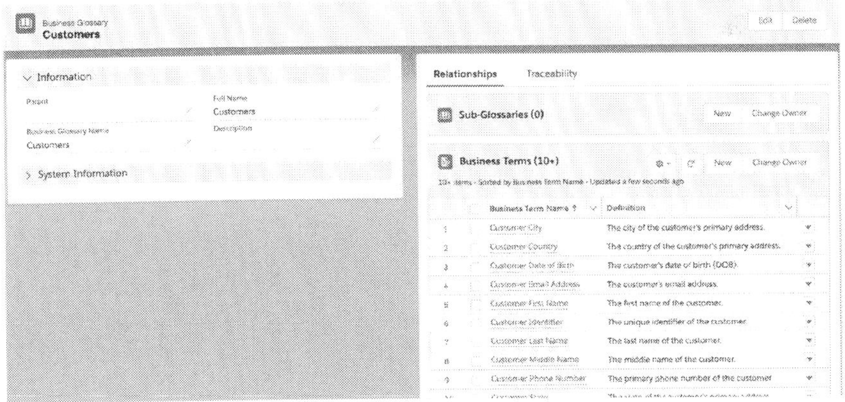

Figure 13.4: Business glossary in YourDataConnect

Any asset in YourDataConnect, including business glossaries and business terms, can have relationships to other assets. For example, Figure 13.5 shows a *Customer Date of Birth* business term mapped to a *DOB* column in a *CUSTOMER* database table.

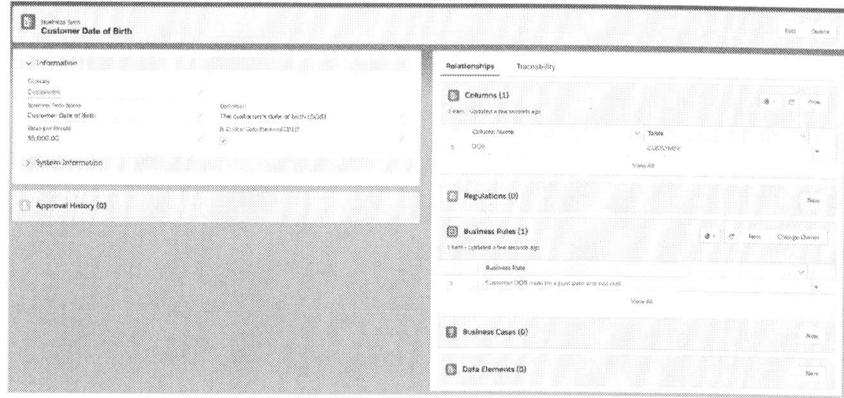

Figure 13.5: Business term related to column in YourDataConnect

Every asset in YourDataConnect has a traceability feature that lets users interactively browse assets and navigate their relationships to other assets visually. Figure 13.6 shows the traceability of the *Customer Date of Birth* business term.

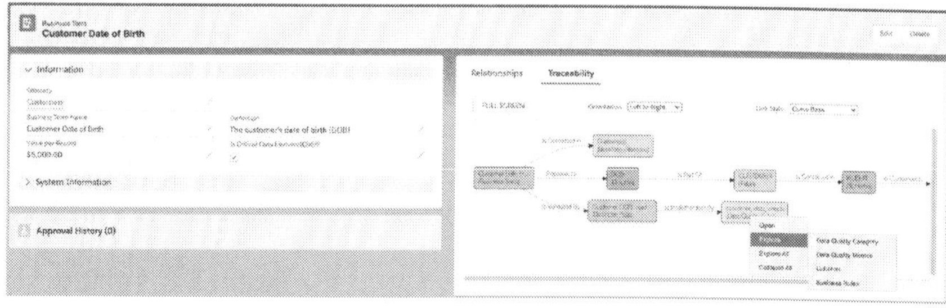

Figure 13.6: Business term traceability in YourDataConnect

Data Catalog

The data catalog enables an organization to build a single view of all technical data assets in the enterprise. Figure 13.7 shows an example of the data catalog. YourDataConnect can ingest metadata from sources including:

- Data lakes
- Databases (relational, NoSQL, and NewSQL)
- BI platforms
- ETL tools
- Artificial intelligence/machine learning platforms

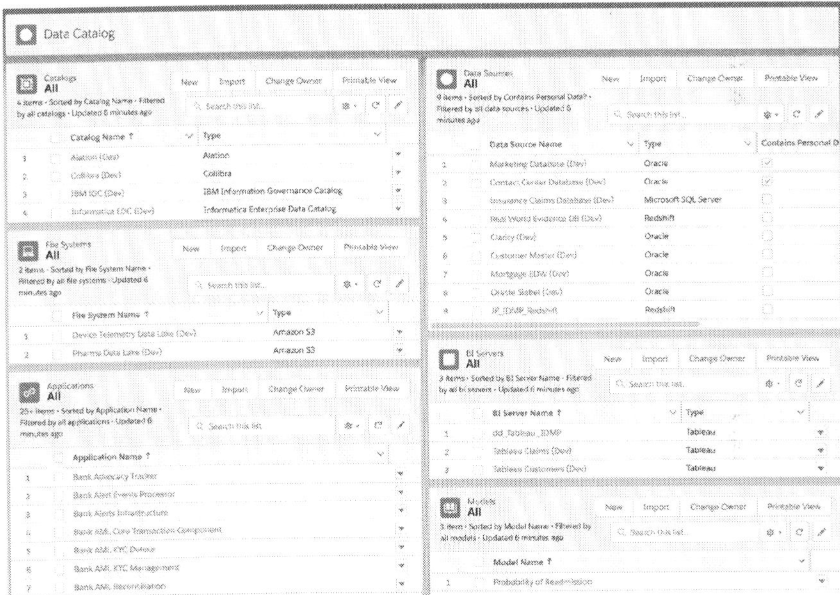

Figure 13.7: Data catalog in YourDataConnect

Data sampling and data profiling can be enabled for data sources as well. Figure 13.8 shows sample data and profiling results for a field in a CSV file stored in Amazon® S3™.

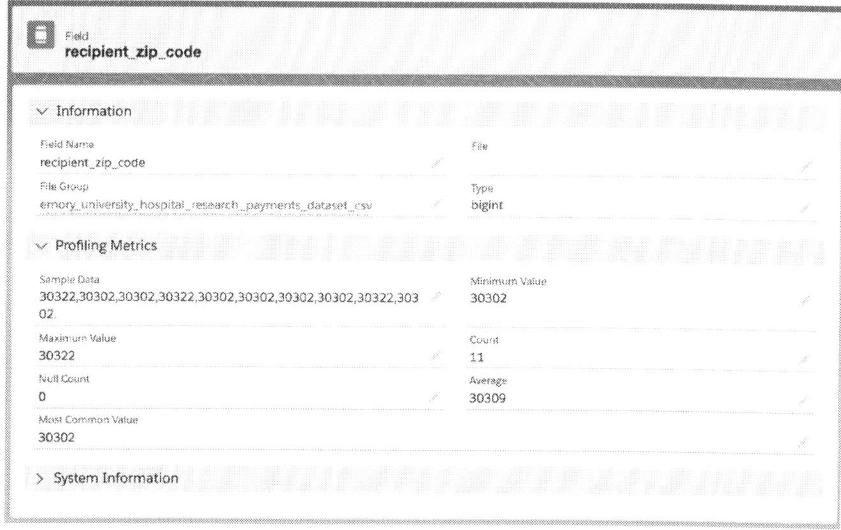

Figure 13.8: Data sampling and data profiling results in YourDataConnect

Data Privacy

YourDataConnect provides a customizable front-end user interface and associated workflows for handling data privacy requests, such as "right-to-know" and "right-to-be-forgotten" requests. A company's customers can submit requests through the user interface shown in Figure 13.9.

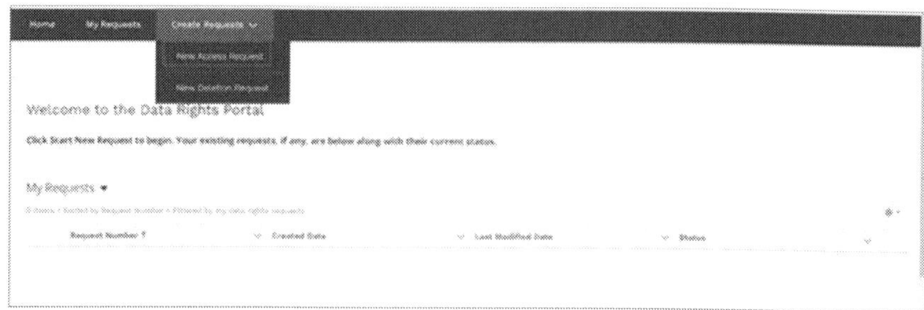

Figure 13.9: Data privacy portal user interface in YourDataConnect

Once the requests are submitted, data owners are assigned tasks by YourDataConnect instructing them to fulfill the request. For example, in Figure 13.10, the owner of the marketing database has a pending task to delete John Doe's personal data from the marketing database.

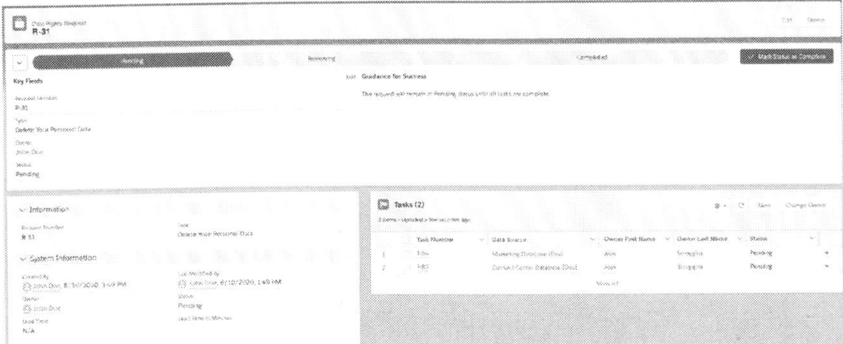

Figure 13.10: Tasks assigned to data owner in YourDataConnect

Once the tasks are completed by all data owners, the requester is notified via email of the actions taken in response to the request, including any relevant exemptions that prevented the action from occurring.

Workflows

YourDataConnect provides several workflows out-of-the-box, allows those workflows to be customized, and supports the creation of new workflows without the need for software development. Customizing or creating workflows is done through a point-and-click interface and requires no coding. Figure 13.11 shows a form for defining a new business term.

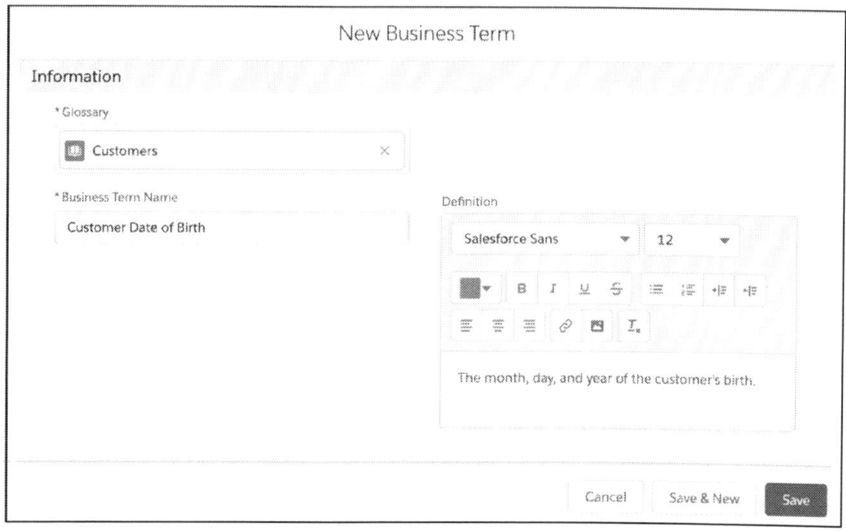

Figure 13.11: New business term form in YourDataConnect

Figure 13.12 shows an email notification sent to a group of approvers requesting approval.

Term "Customer Date of Birth" Submitted for Approval Inbox

Alex Scroggins via wte0ztg0v5x47t.2x-cneteac.ap17.bnc.salesforce.com
to me

Data Stewards,

Alex Scroggins has submitted term "Customer Date of Birth" for your approval.

Please visit the link below to approve or reject this request:
https://yourdataconnect-demo-dev-ed.my.salesforce.com/p/process/ProcessInstanceWorkitemWizardStageManager?id=04i2x000001ayYT

Thank you,
YourDataConnect

Figure 13.12: Approver email notification

Figure 13.13 shows the approval screen for this business term, with options to approve or reject its creation.

Figure 13.14 shows the configuration screen of this workflow. Approval steps are shown, as well as what actions to take for the approval steps. For example, on Data Steward Approval, an email is sent and a status field is updated to Approved. As the figure shows, the approval process can be changed to have more or less functionality without the need to write code

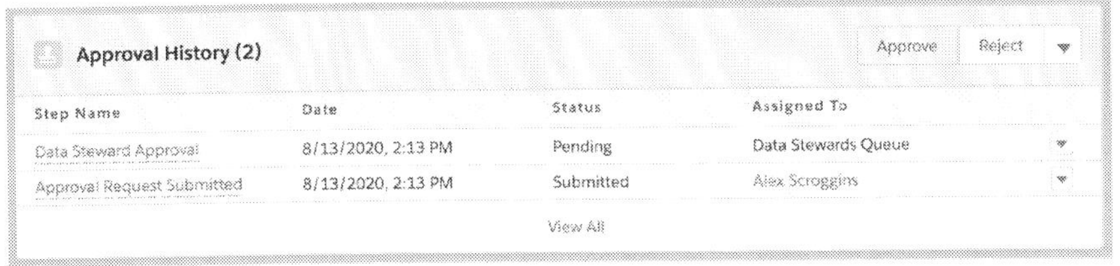

Figure 13.13: Business term approval screen

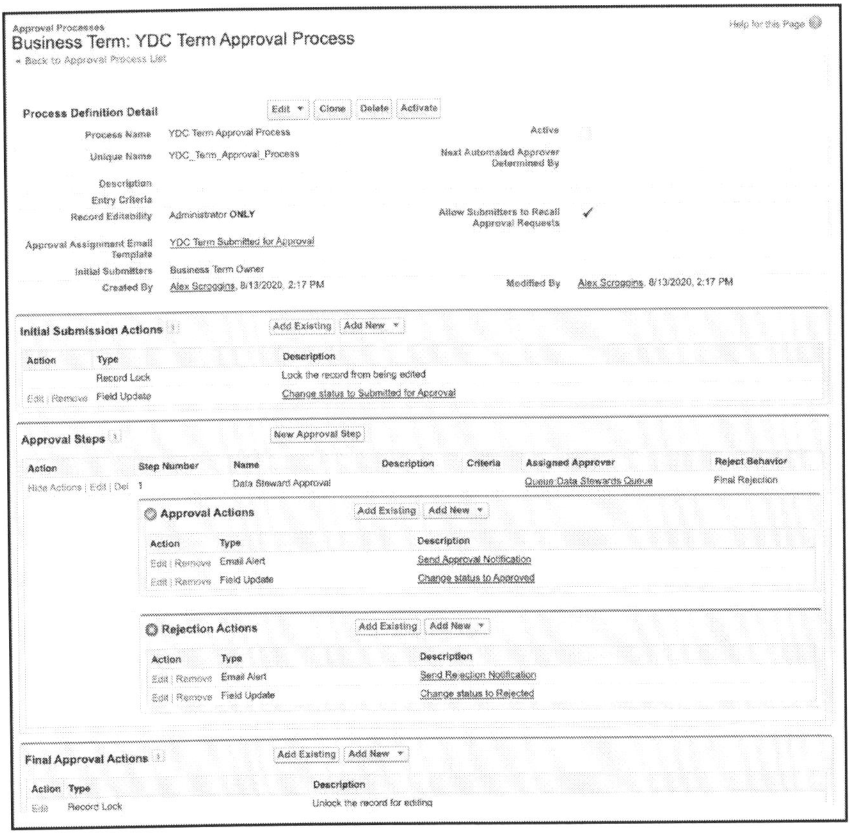

Approval Processes
Business Term: YDC Term Approval Process
« Back to Approval Process List
Help for this Page

Process Definition Detail
Edit | Clone | Delete | Activate

Process Name	YDC Term Approval Process	Active	
Unique Name	YDC_Term_Approval_Process	Next Automated Approver Determined By	
Description			
Entry Criteria			
Record Editability	Administrator ONLY	Allow Submitters to Recall Approval Requests	✓
Approval Assignment Email Template	YDC Term Submitted for Approval		
Initial Submitters	Business Term Owner		
Created By	Alex Scroggins, 8/13/2020, 2:17 PM	Modified By	Alex Scroggins, 8/13/2020, 2:17 PM

Initial Submission Actions
Add Existing | Add New

Action	Type	Description
	Record Lock	Lock the record from being edited
Edit | Remove	Field Update	Change status to Submitted for Approval

Approval Steps
New Approval Step

Action	Step Number	Name	Description	Criteria	Assigned Approver	Reject Behavior
Hide Actions | Edit | Del	1	Data Steward Approval			Queue Data Stewards Queue	Final Rejection

Approval Actions
Add Existing | Add New

Action	Type	Description
Edit | Remove	Email Alert	Send Approval Notification
Edit | Remove	Field Update	Change status to Approved

Rejection Actions
Add Existing | Add New

Action	Type	Description
Edit | Remove	Email Alert	Send Rejection Notification
Edit | Remove	Field Update	Change status to Rejected

Final Approval Actions
Add Existing | Add New

Action	Type	Description
Edit	Record Lock	Unlock the record for editing

Figure 13.14: Business term approval process configuration options in YourDataConnect

or Hypertext Markup Language (HTML). This principle is referred to as "clicks, not code." Approval processes for other objects besides business terms, even custom objects, can be created following the same principle.

Reference Data Management

YourDataConnect contains an operating model with workflows for reference data management. Figure 13.15 shows a sample crosswalk used at a utilities company to map customer types from a customer relationship management (CRM) system to corresponding values in a legacy mainframe system. For instance, in the CRM, industrial customers of the utility are categorized as either "Industrial – Light" or "Industrial – Heavy". However, in the legacy mainframe system, there is only a single classification for industrial customers: "IND". The crosswalk allows customer types to be translated appropriately from the CRM to the mainframe, and vice versa.

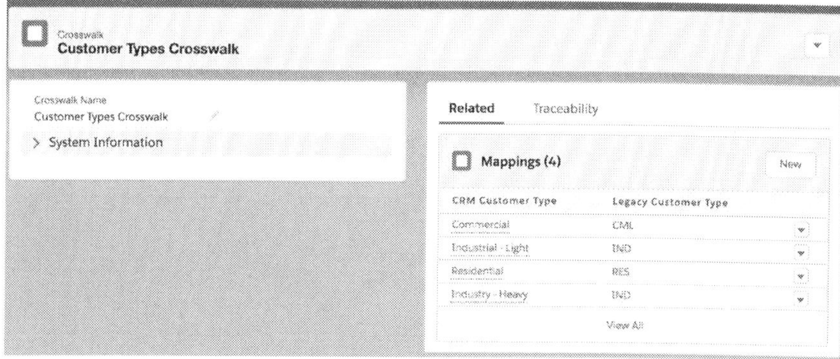

Figure 13.15: Customer type reference data crosswalk in YourDataConnect

Regulatory Compliance

YourDataConnect contains accelerators for compliance with various regulations, such as financial regulations, data privacy regulations, and more. The accelerators include an operating model that includes jurisdiction, regulation, policy, and critical data elements. The accelerators also include specific workflows for assisting with various requirements of the regulations, such as the data privacy workflow shown earlier, in Figures 13.9 and 13.10.

Figure 13.16 shows a regulation for the Children's Online Privacy Protection Act (COPPA), including relevant business terms for that regulation.

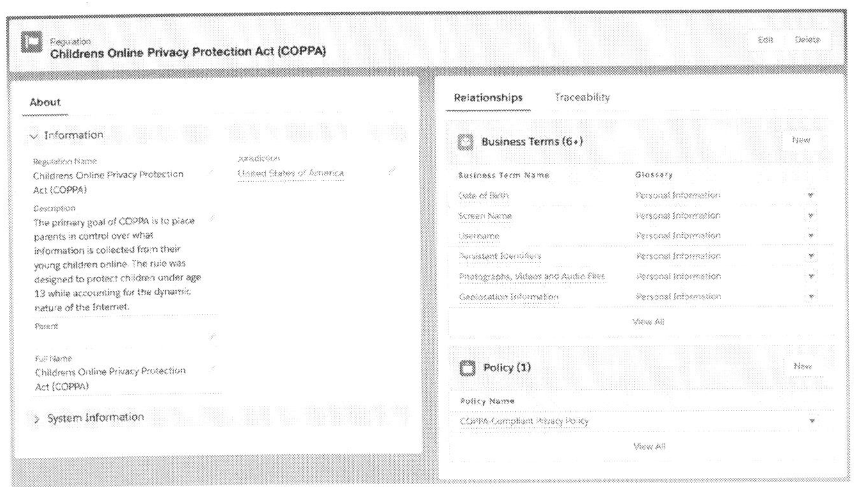

Figure 13.16: COPPA regulation in YourDataConnect

Figure 13.17 shows the traceability of the COPPA regulation, which reveals that some of its CDEs are relevant to other regulations, such as the California Consumer Privacy Act (CCPA).

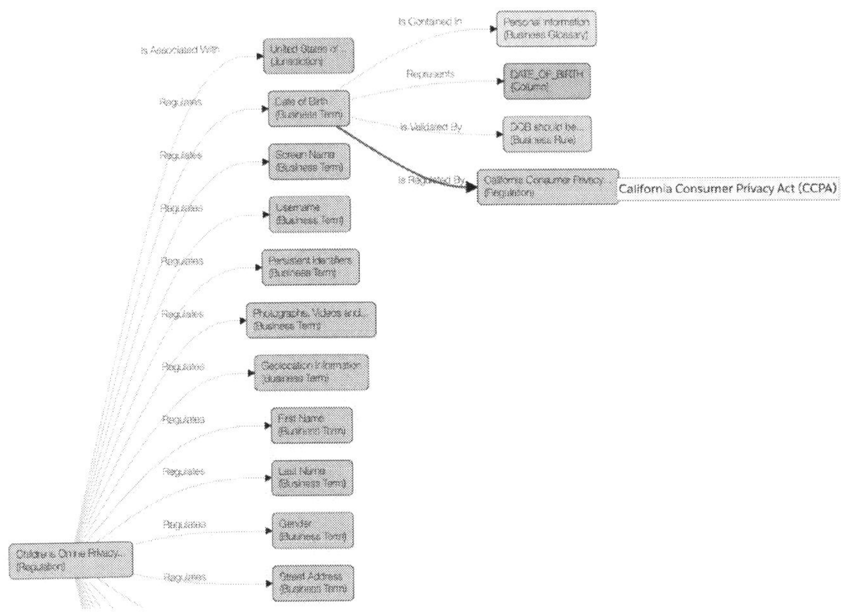

Figure 13.17: COPPA regulation traceability in YourDataConnect

Summary

YourDataConnect is the industry's first SaaS data monetization platform to help organizations capture financial benefits by growing revenues, reducing costs, and managing risk. YourDataConnect offers a number of features, including a data monetization dashboard, a business glossary, data privacy, workflows, reference data management, and regulatory compliance.

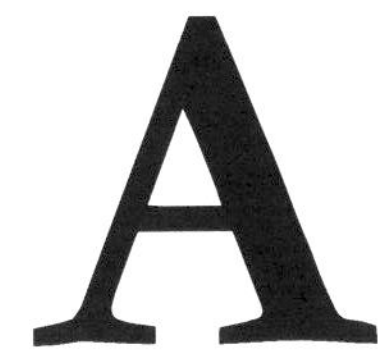

Glossary

Critical data

A set of data or information that is necessary to an organization's operations.

Critical data elements

The 10 to 15 percent of data that is important to a business outcome.

Critical data sets

In the context of data monetization, groupings or collections of data that may cause operational, regulatory, or financial risk if they are not collected or are incorrect, compromised, or used inappropriately.

Data anonymization

The process of removing, scrubbing, and redacting personally identifiable information from data sets to keep the data subject from being identified.

Data architecture

A discipline that sets data standards for data systems as a vision or a model of the eventual interactions between those data systems.[43]

Data category

Logical classification of information to support data governance.

Data governance

The formulation of policy to optimize, secure, and leverage information as an enterprise asset by aligning the objectives of multiple functions.

---

[43] Wikipedia, "Data Architecture," http://en.wikipedia.org/wiki/Data_architecture

Data integration

A process that involves combining data from multiple sources to provide new insights to business users.

Data marketplace

Online catalog of datasets that allows for the internal or external monetization of data.

Data modeling

The process of establishing data models, which use a set of symbols and text to precisely explain a subset of real information to improve communication within the organization and thereby lead to a more flexible and stable application environment.[44]

Data monetization

Cross-functional discipline that draws from best practices in enterprise data management, technology, legal engineering, and finance to leverage data to increase revenues, reduce costs, and manage risk.

Data monetization dashboard

Visual representation of the business benefits of data monetization to executive management.

Data privacy

The process that involves protecting data belonging to an individual or organization.

Data quality management

A discipline that includes methods to measure and improve the quality and integrity of an organization's data.

Data security

The process of avoiding unauthorized access to data.

Data Subject Access Request (DSAR)

Request by a data subject for their personal data in accordance with data privacy regulations such as CCPA and GDPR.

---

[44] Steve Hoberman, *Data Modeling Made Simple*, 2nd ed., Technics Publications, LLC, 2009

Data warehousing and business intelligence

The process of creating a centralized repository of data for reporting and analysis.

Enterprise data management (EDM)

The ability of an organization to precisely define, easily integrate, and effectively retrieve data for both internal applications and external communication.[45] EDM includes a number of disciplines, such as data architecture, data modeling, data integration (extract, transform, load, or ETL), data security, data privacy, master data management, reference data management, data warehousing and business intelligence, information lifecycle management, content management, metadata management, data quality management, data ownership and stewardship, and critical data elements and critical data sets. Strictly speaking, data security and privacy are broader disciplines but have significant interdependencies with enterprise data management and data governance.

Extract, transform, load (ETL)

A process used in data warehousing to extract data from one or more data sources, transform the data, and load the data into a target database.

Information lifecycle management

The process and methodology of managing information through its lifecycle, from creation through disposal, including compliance with legal, regulatory, and privacy requirements.

Jurisdiction

A geographic location where regulations may apply.

Legal engineer

A professional who uses their legal knowledge combined with technological know-how and project management experience to optimize existing products, services, and processes but also to create new solutions to specific problems faced by clients, using a combination of technology and tools.[46]

---

[45] Wikipedia, "Enterprise data management," http://en.wikipedia.org/wiki/Enterprise_data_management

[46] HighQ, part of Thomson Reuters, July 27, 2016 ,"The rise of the legal engineer," https://www.lexology.com/library/detail.aspx?g=f8d9bb92-3779-4bc2-9f1b-7354d416acb1#:~:text=Legal%20engineers%20use%20their%20legal,combination%20of%20technology%20and%20tools

Master data management

The process of establishing a single version of the truth for an organization's critical data entities, such as customers, products, materials, vendors, and chart of accounts.

Metadata management

The management of information that describes the characteristics of any data artifact, such as its name, location, criticality, quality, business rules, and relationships to other data artifacts.

Personal data

Any information relating to an identified or identifiable natural person ("data subject").[47]

Privacy

The "right to be left alone," as defined in a *Harvard Law Review* article entitled "The Right to Privacy," written in 1890 by Louis Brandeis and Samuel Warren. Subsequent regulations and legislation around the world have built on this definition.

Reference data management

The process of managing static data such as country codes, state or province codes, and industry classification codes, which may be placed in lookup tables for reference by other applications across the enterprise.

Sensitive data

Any data that requires security standards to protect its confidentiality and integrity.

Sensitive data management

A discipline that harmonizes the relationship between people, processes, and technology to protect sensitive data.

---

[47] GDPR Article 4, Definitions

B

Acronyms

AML	Anti-Money Laundering
API	Application Programming Interface
APR	Annual Percentage Rate
BHC	Bank Holding Company
BI	Business Intelligence
BSA	Bank Secrecy Act
CASL	Canada's Anti-Spam Legislation
CCAR	Comprehensive Capital Analysis and Review
CCPA	California Consumer Privacy Act
CDE	Critical Data Element
CECL	Current Expected Credit Loss
CFPB	Consumer Financial Protection Bureau
CLA	Consumer Leasing Act
COPPA	Children's Online Privacy Protection Act
CRA	Community Reinvestment Act
CRM	Customer Relationship Management
DFAST	Dodd-Frank Act Stress Test
DPA	Data Protection Act (France)
DSAR	Data Subject Access Request
ECOA	Equal Credit Opportunity Act
EDM	Enterprise Data Management
EFTA	Electronic Fund Transfer Act
EMA	European Medicines Agency
ERP	Enterprise Resource Planning

EU	European Union
FACT	Fair and Accurate Credit Transactions Act of 2003
FASB	Financial Accounting Standards Board (United States)
FCA	Farm Credit Administration
FCRA	Fair Credit Reporting Act
FDA	Food and Drug Administration
FDCPA	Fair Debt Collection Practices Act
FDIC	Federal Deposit Insurance Corporation
FFIEC	Federal Financial Institutions Examination Council
FinCEN	Financial Crimes Enforcement Network
FRB	Federal Reserve Board
FRS	Federal Reserve System
FTC	Federal Trade Commission
GAAP	Generally Accepted Accounting Principles
GDPR	General Data Protection Regulation (European Union)
GL	General Ledger
GLBA	Gramm-Leach-Bliley Act
GUDID	Global Unique Device Identification Database
HMDA	Home Mortgage Disclosure Act
HPA	Homeowners Protection Act
HPML	Higher-Priced Mortgage Loan
HTML	Hypertext Markup Language
HUD	Department of Housing and Urban Development
IDMP	Identification of Medicinal Products
IEEPA	International Emergency Economic Powers Act
IFRS	International Financial Reporting Standard
IHC	Intermediate Holding Company
ISO	International Organization for Standardization
IVTS	Informal Value Transfer Systems
LEI	Legal Entity Identifier
LOB	Line of Business
MDM	Master Data Management
MDR	Medical Device Regulation (European Union)
MLO	Mortgage Loan Originator

NCUA	National Credit Union Administration
OCC	Office of the Comptroller of the Currency
OFAC	Office of Foreign Assets Control
OTS	Office of Thrift Supervision
PCD	Purchased Credit Deteriorated
PDPA	Personal Data Protection Act (Singapore)
PII	Personally Identifiable Information
PIPEDA	Personal Information Protection and Electronic Documents Act
PMI	Private Mortgage Insurance
PRC	People's Republic of China
RACI	Responsibility Assignment Matrix
RESPA	Real Estate Settlement Procedures Act
REST	Representational State Transfer
SaaS	Software-as-a-Service
SAFE	Secure and Fair Enforcement for Mortgage Licensing
SAR	Suspicious Activity Report
SDM	Sensitive Data Management
SDN	Specially Designated Nationals
SLA	Service Level Agreement
SME	Subject Matter Expert
SPOR	Substance, Product, Organization, and Referential
SSI	Sectoral Sanctions Identifications
SWOT	Strengths, Weaknesses, Opportunities, and Threats
TFI	Office of Terrorism and Financial Intelligence
TILA	Truth in Lending Act
TISA	Truth in Savings Act
UDAAPs	Unfair, Deceptive, or Abusive Acts or Practices
UDI	Unique Device Identifier
URL	Uniform Resource Locator
VPPA	Video Privacy Protection Act
XML	Extensible Markup Language

Made in the USA
Middletown, DE
19 September 2020

20181461R00073